Citizenship and Globalisation

CITIZENSHIP AND GLOBALISATION

ZEENAT ARA
SHUBHRA PANT KOTHARI

ABHIJEET PUBLICATIONS
DELHI 110094

ABHIJEET PUBLICATIONS
2/46 Tukhmeerpur Extension
Delhi-110 094
Phone: 011-22960492, 65698474
E-mail: abhijeetpublication@gmail.com

CITIZENSHIP AND GLOBALISATION

First Published 2010

ISBN 978-93-80031-98-9

PRINTED IN INDIA

Published by J.K. Singh for Abhijeet Publications, Delhi-110 094, Lasertypeset by Gaurav Graphics, New Delhi and Printed at Himanshu Printers, Delhi.

Preface

Globalisation has been the most important phenomenon in the economic political and cultural history of the last century and continues to be so. There have been several forms of Globalisation which have become a topical issue ever since Bretton Woods Conference leading to the formation of international economic institutions.

Globalization is the term used to characterize the processes of growing interconnection and inter dependence in the modern world. It is generated by growing international economic, cultural and political cooperation and as well as by the need to respond together to global problems, which can be solved only on global scale.

The implications of globalization for a national economy are many. Globalisation has intensified interdependence and competition between economic in the world market. This is reflected in Interdependence in regard to trading in goods and services and in movement of capital. As a result domestic economic developments are not determined entirely by domestic policies and market conditions. It is thus clear that a globalizing economy, while formulating and evaluating its domestic policy cannot afford to ignore the possible actions and reactions of policies and developments in the rest of the world. This constrained the policy option available to the government which implies loss of policy autonomy to some extent, in decision-making at the national level.

Globalization is in many ways undermining national-citizenship but perhaps this is because national-citizenship is anachronistic in the world today. One hundred years ago it was the dominant form, although it is debatable as to whether it actually ever truly existed, but now we need a more universal concept, perhaps 'post national' as argued by SOYSAL, differentiated as argued by Young or multicultural citizenship as proposed by KYMILICKA. It is not simply global pressures that are undermining national citizenship but they certainly are helping it into the history books.

This book is a culmination of discussions and deliberations that took place formally or informally between the two authors. This book would not have seen beam of light without the guidance and help of academicians and organizations. Therefore we consider it extremely important to acknowledge them all for their significant considerations for the book.

We sincerely thank and acknowledge Dr. Anil Dutta Mishra and Dr. Sweta Mishra as this book is, indeed, a result of affable cooperation and encouragement of both in the accomplishment of this book.

We are thankful to Dr. S.K. Jolly, Principal, Shyama Prasad Mukherjee College, University of Delhi and Dr. S.A. Hamideen, Principal, Zakir Hussain P.G. Delhi

College (Evening), University of Delhi for her motivational deliberation.

We are thankful to the staff of the Nehru Memorial Museum and Library, the Indian Institute of Public Administration and its library, the Ratan Tata Library, the DSC, WSDC Library, CWDS Library, DSA, Department of Poltical Science, JNU, SRL, Centre of Political Studies, JNU.

We are thankful to our publisher, Abhijeet, who managed to bring out the book on time.

We thank our family and friends for their emotional and inspirational support in the accomplishment of this work.

Zeenat Ara

Shubhra Pant Kothari

Contents

1

Globalization

Globalization in a literal sense is international integration. It can be described as a process by which the people of the world are unified into a single society. This process is a combination of economic, technological, sociocultural and political forces.

Globalization, as a term, is very often used to refer to economic globalization, that is integration of national economies into the international economy through trade, foreign direct investment, capital flows, migration, and spread of technology.

The word globalization in what Noam Chomsky calls a doctrinal sense is also used to describe the particular neoliberal form of economic globalization.

Globalization is also defined as the internationalization of everything related to different countries; Internationalization however, as a contrasted phenomenon, differs from globalization in that Global is commonly used as a synonym for "international", however such usage is typically incorrect as "global" implies "one world" as a single unit, while "international" (between nations) recognizes that different peoples, cultures, languages, nations, borders, economies, and ecosystems exist.

The process of globalization had its origins in Europe, through the Portuguese, Spanish, Dutch, French, and English territorial and maritime expansion into all habitable continents, and included the discovery and colonization of the New World.

In the arena of social policy it may refer to a relaxation of laws restricting for example divorce, abortion, homosexuality or drugs.

Most often, the term is used to refer to economic liberalization, especially trade liberalization or capital market liberalization.

According to the *Oxford English Dictionary*, the word 'globalization' was first employed in 1930, to denote a holistic view of human experience in education.[1] An early description of globalization was penned by the American entrepreneur-turned-minister Charles Taze Russell who coined the term 'corporate giants' in 1897,[2] although it was not until the 1960s that the term began to be widely used by economists and other social scientists. The term has since then achieved widespread use in the mainstream press by the later half of the 1980s. Since its inception, the concept of globalization has inspired numerous competing definitions and interpretations, with antecedents dating back to the great movements of trade and empire across Asia and the Indian Ocean from the 15th century onwards.[3]

The United Nations ESCWA has written that globalization "is a widely-used term that can be defined in a number of different ways. When used in an economic context, it refers to the reduction and removal of barriers between national borders in order to facilitate the flow of goods, capital, services and labor... although considerable barriers remain to the flow of labor... Globalization is not a new phenomenon. It began in the late nineteenth century, but it slowed down during the period from the start of the First World War until the third quarter of the twentieth century. This slowdown can be attributed to the inward-looking policies pursued by a number of countries in order to protect their respective industries... however, the pace of globalization picked up rapidly during the fourth quarter of the twentieth century..."[4]

Saskia Sassen writes that "a good part of globalization consists of an enormous variety of micro-processes that begin to denationalize what had been constructed as national— whether policies, capital, political subjectivity, urban spaces, temporal frames, or any other of a variety of dynamics and domains."[5]

Tom J. Palmer of the Cato Institute defines globalization as "the diminution or elimination of state-enforced restrictions on exchanges across borders and the increasingly integrated and complex global system of production and exchange that has emerged as a result."[6]

Thomas L. Friedman has examined the impact of the "flattening" of the world, and argues that globalized trade, outsourcing, supply-chaining, and political forces have changed the world permanently, for both better and worse. He also argues that the pace of globalization is quickening and will continue to have a growing impact on business organization and practice.[7]

Noam Chomsky argues that the word globalization is also used, in a doctrinal sense, to describe the neoliberal form of economic globalization.[8]

Finally, Takis Fotopoulos argues that globalization is the result of systemic trends manifesting the market economy's grow-or-die dynamic, following the rapid expansion of transnational corporations. Because these trends have not been offset effectively by counter-tendencies that could have emanated from trade-union action and other forms of political activity, the outcome has been globalisation. This is a multi-faceted and irreversible phenomenon within the system of the market economy and it is expressed as: economic globalisation, namely, the opening and deregulation of commodity, capital and labour markets which led to the present form of neoliberal globalisation; political globalisation, i.e., the emergence of a transnational elite and the phasing out of the all powerful-nation state of the statist period; cultural globalisation, i.e., the worldwide homogenisation of culture; ideological globalisation; technological globalisation; social globalisation.[9]

The human society around the world, over a period of time, has established greater contact, but the pace has increased rapidly since the mid 1980's. The term globalization means international integration. It includes an array of social, political and economic changes. Unimaginable progress in modes of communications, transportation and computer technology have given the process a new lease of life.

The world is more interdependent now than ever before. Multinational companies manufacture products across many countries and sell to consumers across the globe. Money, technology and raw materials have broken the International barriers. Not only products and finances, but also ideas and cultures have breached the national boundaries. Laws, economies and social movements have become international in nature and not only the Globalization of the Economy but also the Globalization of Politics, Culture and Law is the order of the day. The formation of General Agreement on Tariffs and Trade (GATT), International Monetary Fund and the concept of free trade has boosted globalization.

Dimensions of Globalisation

The economic aspects stressed in globalization are trade, investment and migration. The globalization of trade entails that human beings have greater access to an array of goods and services never seen before in human history. From German cars, to Colombian coffee, from Chinese clothing, to Egyptian cotton, from American music to Indian software, human beings may be able to purchase a wide range of goods and services. The globalization of investment takes place through Foreign Direct Investment, where multinational companies directly invest assets in a foreign country, or by indirect investment where individuals and institutions purchase and sell financial assets of other countries. Free migration allows individuals to find employment in jurisdictions where there are labor shortages.

The political aspects of globalization are evidenced when governments create international rules and institutions to deal with issues such as trade, human rights, and the environment. Among the new institutions and rules that have come to fruition as a result of globalization are the World Trade Organization, the Euro currency, the North American Free Trade Agreement, to name a few. Whether a government is to consciously open itself to cross-border links, is the central question of this aspect.

Social activist and non-profit organizations such as Amnesty International and Greenpeace are also becoming more global in scope. Some of these organizations take issue with the economic and political aspects of globalization as they fear that economic interests either subvert the nation state in its ability to protect its citizens from economic exploitation, or support governments that violate the human rights of their citizens.

Cultural global ties also grow through globalization as news ideas and fashions through trade, travel and media move around the globe at lightning speed. Global brands such as Coca-Cola, Nike & Sony serve as common reference to consumers all over the World. An individual in China enjoys the same soft drink as an individual in Puerto Rico—at opposite ends of the globe. However, these ties may also cause strains: for example Western Ideas of freedom of expression may clash with Islamic views on Religious tolerance. And if not strains, critics contend this is really an imposition of cultural imperialism in order to preserve economic interests.

The other aspect of globalization is the revolutionary change in technology, particularly in transport and communication, which ostensibly creates a global village. In 1850 it took nearly a year to sail around the World. Now you can fly around the world in a day, send an email anywhere almost instantly, or be part of the 1.5 billion viewers watching the final match of the World Cup. Transportation costs have come down as result of technological advances that make foreign markets more accessible to trade. Tuna caught in the North Atlantic may be served the next day at a Sushi restaurant in Japan. Finally, billions of dollars in assets and currencies are exchanged daily around the globe by electronic means at virtually no cost. Globalization spreads everything.

Globalism, if the concept is reduced to its economic aspects, can be said to contrast with economic nationalism and protectionism. It is related to laissez-faire capitalism and neoliberalism.

It shares a number of characteristics with internationalization and is often used interchangeably, although some prefer to use globalization to emphasize the erosion of the nation-state or national boundaries.

Making connections between places on a global scale. Today, more and more places around the world are connected to each other in ways that were previously unimaginable. In geography, this process is known as complex connectivity, where more and more places are being connected in more and more ways.

In its cultural form, globalization has been a label used to identify attempts to erode the national cultures of Europe, and subsume them into a global culture whose members will be much easier to manipulate through mass media and controlled governments. In this context, massive legal or illegal immigration has been allowed, mainly in European countries.

The formation of a global village closer contact between different parts of the world, with increasing possibilities of personal exchange, mutual understanding and friendship between "world citizens", and creation of a global civilization.

There are four aspects to economic globalization, referring to four different flows across boundaries, namely flows of goods/services, i.e. 'free trade' (or at least freer trade), flows of people (migration), of capital, and of technology. A consequence of economic globalization is increasing relations among members of an industry in different parts of the world (globalization of an industry), with a corresponding erosion of national sovereignty in the economic sphere. The IMF defines globalization as the growing economic interdependence of countries worldwide through increasing volume and variety of cross-border transactions in goods and services, freer international capital flows, and more rapid and widespread diffusion of technology (IMF, World Economic Outlook, May, 1997). The World Bank defines globalization as the "Freedom and ability of individuals and firms to initiate voluntary economic transactions with residents of other countries".

Effects of Globalization

Developed nations have outsourced manufacturing and white collar jobs. That means less jobs for their people. This has happened because manufacturing work is outsourced to developing nations like China where the cost of manufacturing goods and wages are lower. Programmers, editors, scientists and accountants have lost their jobs due to outsourcing to cheaper locations like India.

Globalization has led to exploitation of labor. Prisoners and child workers are used to work in inhumane conditions. Safety standards are ignored to produce cheap goods.

Job insecurity, Earlier people had stable, permanent jobs. Now people live in constant dread of losing their jobs to competition. Increased job competition has led to reduction in wages and consequently lower standards of living.

Terrorists have access to sophisticated weapons enhancing their ability to inflict damage. Terrorists use the Internet for communicating among themselves.

Companies have set up industries causing pollution in countries with poor regulation of pollution.

Fast food chains like McDonalds and KFC are spreading in the developing world. People are consuming more junk food from these joints which has an adverse impact on their health.

The benefits of globalization is not universal. The rich are getting richer and the poor are becoming poorer.

Bad apects of foreign cultures are affecting the local cultures through TV and the Internet.

Enemy nations can spread propaganda through the Internet.

Deadly diseases like HIV/AIDS are being spread by travellers to the remotest corners of the globe.

Local industries are being taken over by foreign multinationals.

The increase in prices has reduced the governments ability to sustain social welfare schemes in developed countries.

There is increase in human trafficking.

Multinatonal Companies and corporations which were previously restricted to commercial activities are increasingly influencing political decisions.

However it has the other side also...

Globalization has created the concept of outsourcing. Work such as software development, customer support, marketing, accounting and insurance is outsourced to developing countries like India. So the company that outsourced the work enjoys the benefit of lower costs because the wages in developing countries is far lower than that of developed countries. The workers in the developing countries get employment. Developing countries get access to the latest technology.

Increased competition forces companies to lower prices. This benefits the end consumers. Increased media coverage draws the attention of the world to human right violations. This leads to improvement in human rights.

The implications of globalisation for a national economy are many. Globalisation has intensified interdependence and competition between economies in the world market. This is reflected in Interdependence in regard to trading in goods and services and in movement of capital. As a result domestic economic developments are not determined entirely by domestic policies and market conditions. Rather, they are influenced by both domestic and international policies and economic conditions. It is thus clear that a globalising economy, while formulating and evaluating its domestic policy cannot afford to ignore the possible actions and reactions of policies and developments in the rest of the world. This constrained the policy option available to the government which implies loss of policy autonomy to some extent, in decision-making at the national level.

Globalization is not a fair game, of course. Those with giant economies get the lion's share of the 'collective' decision-making. Those with more money and global outlook tend to have influential media, also with global outlook. In both scenarios, small countries are lost between desperately trying to negotiate a better economic standing for themselves, while hopelessly trying to maintain their cultural identity, which defined their people, generation after generation throughout history.

NOTES

1. W. Boyd & M. M. MacKenzie. *Towards New Education, IV'*, (1930). p. 350
2. *The Battle of Armageddon*, October, 1897, pp. 365–370.
3. A.G. Hopkins, ed. *Globalization in World History*, Norton, (2004), pp. 4-8.
4. Summary of the Annual Review of Developments in Globalization and Regional Integration in the Countries of the ESCWA Region by the United Nations Economic and Social Commission for Western Asia.
5. Sassen, Saskia (2006). Territory, Authority, Rights: From Medieval to Global Assemblages. Princeton University Press.
6. Globalization Is Great! by Tom G. Palmer, Senior Fellow, Cato Institute.
7. Friedman, Thomas L. "The Dell Theory of Conflict Prevention". Emergin: A Reader. Ed. Barclay Barrios. Boston: Bedford, St. Martins, 2008.
8. ZNet, Corporate Globalization, Korea and International Affairs, Noam Chomsky interviewed by Sun Woo Lee, Monthly Joong Ang, 22 February 2006.
9. "Globalisation, the reformist Left and the Anti-Globalisation 'Movement'", Takis Fotopoulos, *Democracy & Nature: The International Journal of Inclusive Democracy*, Vol. 7, No. 2, (July 2001).

2

Citizenship and Globalisation

The idea that citizenship exists in uneasy relationship with globalization is intuitively plausible. Citizenship derives from the existence of a community of people, a polity, embedded in a geographically bounded nation state recognized by other nations and with boundaries and laws upheld, if necessary, by force.

Globalization, on the other hand, is a phenomenon. It has political, economic, socio-cultural and technological dimensions[1], and refers to integration and inter-connectedness across national boundaries along these dimensions. Because goods, services, ideas, and people have always moved, to some extent, around the globe, references to globalization today speak to a change in the magnitude of such movement. It is a phenomenon of increased interconnectedness—increased flows of goods, services, people, and ideas through traditional as well as new channels. This increase has made the relationship of citizen and the nation state more complex.

Current globalization results from the global spread of capitalism, by internationalization of functions of production, and by changes in communications technology. Scholars differ on precise definitions of globalization, but there is consensus that it involves blurring of boundaries. In this paper, "globalization" will refer to "a cluster of related changes that are increasing the interconnectedness of the world. These changes are occurring in, but not limited to, economic, technological, cultural, and political realms. Furthermore, globalization is not restricted to merely enhancing the interdependence of already existing entities or the intensification of established networks or flows, but is also creating or facilitating the creation of new ones."[2]

Two aspects of globalization have implications for citizenship. First, the movement of people across national boundaries to live and work calls into question issues of national identity and belonging, of membership in a polity, and of the rights that accrue to that membership. Second, a hallmark of globalization is the existence of transnational and multinational organizations that are overlays on national sovereignty. These exist in parallel with the nation state and both complicate and diffuse the rights and privileges that accrue to citizenship.

While globalization is not a new phenomenon in the history of the nation state, three aspects of its current manifestation are new and create unique pressures on sovereignty and on citizenship. Firstly, travel has become more rapid and relatively inexpensive, making movement around the globe by individuals, goods, capital, and groups easier and more widespread than ever, and intensifying globalization.[3]

Transnationalism, defined as maintenance of strong, enduring political, social, and economic ties by migrants to their homelands, has become a sufficiently significant phenomenon[4] where production and consumption occur on a global scale. Secondly, computer and telecommunications technology facilitate capital flows around the world and increase the interconnectedness of individuals, ideas, and culture to an unprecedented extent. Foreign-born residents in the United States can keep close contact with their countries of origin through the internet and with satellite technology, often watch the same television programming as they would in their home countries. The ability of individuals to straddle two cultures for long periods of time has never been greater.

Finally, the hegemony of the United States through institutions such as the World Bank and the International Monetary Fund (IMF) creates new mechanisms for constraints on the sovereignty of national governments.

While our first instinct is to view with alarm the idea of international hegemonic pressure on national governments, the story is complicated. In some cases, pressures created by the global spread of capitalism have led governments in developing countries to undertake reforms that strengthened their institutions and democracies.

This chapter will focus on a conceptual framework for the tensions between citizenship and globalization in its current expression. It will also contrast the impact of globalization on citizenship in the world today as compared to globalization during the last immense beckon of immigration at the turn of the 20th century.

CITIZENSHIP, THE NATION-STATE, AND GLOBALIZATION

Culture and National Identity

An extensive academic literature explores the nature of culture and national identity, its relationship to nation states, and to the rights of citizenship which derive from membership in such states. Social scientists debate the extent to which culture and identity is primordial, essential, fixed and given by nationality, ethnicity, and religion. Samuel Huntington, in his book, Clash of Civilizations, is a prominent proponent of this view[5]. An alternative view is of culture and identity as fluid and socially constructed. This view argues that individuals have "any number of identities. Some of these identities intersect or collide with others, and all vary in salience across time and across contexts."[6] And, importantly, this view holds identity to be malleable, shifting across time and place for individuals and for societies.[7]

The Nation and Citizens

A nation is more than a political boundary. It embodies a sense of shared identity and history. Distinguishing between "a nation as a community of citizens from other forms of historical or cultural collectives (ethnies) and from the state"[8] is necessary to specific discussion of citizenship. The following definition of a nation state is useful:

> Like any political unit, the nation is defined by its sovereignty, exercised internally to integrate the populations that it includes and, externally, to assert itself as an historical subject in a global order founded

on the existence and relations between politically constituted nations. But its uniqueness is that it integrates populations in a community of citizens, whose existence legitimates the internal and external action of the state.[9]

An integrated community of citizens confers legitimacy, or nationhood, on the state, but if historical and cultural identities are antecedents of the political form of the state, the salience of these antecedents is bound to increase during periods of flux. Culture and identity matter when considering globalization because they impact the extent to which globalization's blurring of boundaries affects the cohesion of the community of citizens and therefore legitimacy of the nation state.

They also matter because, as will be discussed below, they inform conceptions of the citizen, that are manifest in laws governing membership in the polity—who has standing and what rights accrued to standing. Thus, culture and identity that transcend national boundaries have implications for individual and collective understanding of the community of citizens and directly raises the question of who is "us" and who is "them" within the political boundaries of the nation state. If identity is fixed, then migration of diverse people, culture, and values across political boundaries leads to disintegration of the community of citizens and is an assault on the nation state. In this context, globalization erodes the congruence between the boundaries of the nation (the community of citizens) and the state (the territorial political boundary).

If, on the other hand, identity is fluid and malleable globalization might alter the specific "character" of the community of citizens, but the nation state can be understood as a more robust entity, capable of evolving and adapting. Further, where a nation state is in developmental time is likely to matter to how it is impacted by globalization. Nations go through a dynamic process of integrating its populations into a community of citizens during which there emerges a sense of common goals, a critical mass of common practices and beliefs, and, most importantly, legitimate social and political institutions.[10]

As Dominique Schnapper states in *Community of Citizens*, "The term integration ... is not a matter of an irenic process. On the contrary, it is normally by means of internal violence—by reducing political and cultural particularisms—and external violence—by wars—which the processes of national integration have occurred."[11] Ancient nation states have generally undergone a more thorough process of integration and will be impacted differently by globalization than "developmentally younger" nations.

The years since the Cold War have seen remarkable political and economic flux.

Representative events include the emergence and suspension of nation states, creation of the supranational European Union, unprecedented global economic integration, resurrection of religious fundamentalism and ethnic rivalries, and augmented human mobility around the globe. International labor mobility has resulted in large numbers of people living and working in countries of which they are not citizens.[12]

Human society has become more multifaceted. Individuals visage greater alternatives in deciding where to live and work, making decisions in the context of social and economic networks that extent national boundaries. These networks strengthen ties to people's countries of origin and diminish the extent to which non-residents of country perceive themselves as members of the community of citizens in their countries of residence. Therefore, the structure of communities of citizens within geographically bounded space has been undermined by globalization.[13]

Citizenship Beyond Nation-State

The nation state has been a principal classifying mechanism of human society. But other dimensions of human association—social and political causes, culture, ethnicity, and religion—are increasing in salience and complexity within the boundaries of nation states. The consequences of increased humar. societies are intricate. One way that current globalization enlarges societies and undermines the centrality of the community of citizens is the extent to which people with limited access to the civil, political and social rights of citizenship in the countries of their birth can more easily "vote with the feet" and move across national boundaries in search of a better life.

At first glimpse, the individuals, families, and communities of the transnational workers or laborers do get advantage but at the costs of their political and economic rights of their native countries.

Has the process of out-migration helped the governments to assimilate human society by providing political and economic rights to all? Are there contradictions in the assertion of rights and responsibilities at the global level vis-à-vis regional, national and local level?

GLOBAL CITIZENSHIP

Investigating these questions, we move further to discuss global citizenship. Democracy and globalization are pertinent to modernity:

> The democratic nation is weakened because its sovereignty in the world of politically constituted nations is continually more limited. It is weakened because the political project by which it integrated various populations has been exhausted. National reality has been steadily transformed into a community of work, culture, and the redistribution of wealth. The bond between men becomes less civic than utilitarian or instrumental. Democracy is born under a national form, but the ambition of giving a substantive content to the formal equality of law – embedded in the very values of democratic legitimacy – and the logic of production both risk permanently enfeebling the political project which lay at the foundation of the nation.[14]

Rights which nations afford their citizens fall along a gamut, with liberal democracies at one end and despotic dictatorships at the other. Large numbers of people live with limited citizenship rights under ineffective and/or corrupt governments. While nation states exist in more or less permissible uniformity to one another, citizenship does not bestow equal benefits across or even within states.

Marshall, in his influential work on *citizenship and social class* articulated three key attributes of citizenship as including equality of political, civil, and social rights. His work has been widely accepted in Western political thought. According to him:

> Citizenship has three aspects, namely, that citizens

have a say in political decision making; access to courts of law that are manned by co-citizens who judge according to rules that equally apply to all citizens; and a guarantee of minimum socioeconomic conditions of existence. Citizenship is a matter of emancipation, of successively realizing these threes aspects of political, legal, and socio-economic participation for all people who find themselves on the territory of the state.[15]

Political and civil rights, achieved in western liberal democracies during the 18th and 19th centuries are today a matter of legal definition and whether citizens have equal standing in the law is relatively straight forward to determine. Even today, social rights are more indistinct concept and there is incongruity over whether they relate to equality of outcome or equality of opportunity. Access to social rights has been the domain of the 20th century and nation states vary extremely in the extent to which social rights have been established or are considered legitimate. In the United States, the concept of broadly defined social rights is far from universally accepted.[16]

A corollary concept to the rights of citizenship encoded in the nation state is that of the citizen itself. One view is of the citizen as liberal-individualist, a responsible individual who can make choices and accept the consequences of those choices. Another is of the citizen-communitarian, part of a mutually connected people with a responsibility to help each other out. A third is of the citizen as republican, as a member of a proud public community.[17]

Lister attaches the notion of 'global citizenship' with a 'multi-layered conception' of citizenship itself with states acknowledging the importance of human rights and international law.[18] Each stratum, if it is democratically constructed, strengthens the other stratum. Global citizenship does not operate against the regional, national and local identities as it is concerned with all human agencies.

Heater argues that a 'singular concept' of citizenship has rupture its boundaries and it is true that dual citizenship represents a much more tranquil view of the question so that a person can exercise state-centered citizenship rights in more than one country.[19] He compresses the case for flexible and flowing notion of citizenship by having voluntary association in civil society. Heater stressed that civil society offers a useful and even superior option to traditional citizenship.[20]

Hence, it could be laid out that the notion of a world or global citizen cannot stipulate rights and responsibilities with accuracy that citizenships set out in written or unwritten constitutions can do. Celebrating the Kantian argument for world government, Heater sympathise towards the concept of 'global citizen', stressing for the need of a transfer of civil allegiance from the state to the universal polity.[21] The ideal of cosmopolitan citizenship is the condition in which all human beings have equal recognition as co-legislators within a 'global kingdom of ends.'[22]

Soysal on the other hand emphasises upon national and citizenship identities to be unimaginative and unthinkable without the state. The identity of personhood defined in the human rights discourse moves beyond both citizenship and the state.

Conceptions of the citizen are important because the blurring of boundaries engendered by globalization have implications for the nation state and for the individual citizen.

CONCLUSION

The malleability of Globalisation is being tested. Significant extension of the global community includes diverse races, cultures, religions, and ethnicities. In addition, social rights and communitarian citizenship are also very much in change. The national sphere of influence has become relevant. Following quote speaks to the challenge to citizenship which globalization poses:

> What, if anything, connects nationalist politics to the spread of liberal democratic ideals and institutions? We need to answer that question in order to begin thinking about the extent to which nationalism and the nation-sate will survive the challenge of globalist theory and practice. For globalism relies heavily on the hegemony of liberal democratic ideologies, as well as on processes of cultural and economic integration. If liberal democratic ideals and institutions promote nationalist politics in some way, then the globalist challenge to the nation-state may undermine itself in at least one important way.[23]

Lesson Learnt

- The concept of citizenship has moved beyond from its original state of being membership of the state.
- Citizenship and Globalisation involves a process of change that is evolutionary and revolutionary, so it is important not to overlap both the concepts.

- Cosmopolitan citizenship demands to extend the whole world as a whole, so that people are not merely citizens of a particular country, but citizens of the globe.
- For Global citizenship to be made plausible, the notion of citizenship needs to be separated from the state.

QUESTIONS

1. Citizenship and Globalization involves a process of change that is evolutionary and revolutionary. Explain.
2. Is the notion of citizenship distinct from the State? Critically examine.
3. Critically analyse the concept of Citizenship and its relation with Globalization.

NOTES

1. Croucher, Shiela L., *Globalization and Belonging, The Politics of Identity in a Changing World,* Rowman & Littlefield Publishers, Inc., Lanham Maryland, 2004, p. 10.
2. *Ibid.*, p. 13.
3. *Ibid.*, p. 22.
4. Levitt, Peggy, Josh DeWind and Steven Vertovec, "International Perspectives on Transnational Migration: An Introduction", *International Migration Review,* Volume 37, Number 3, Fall 2003, p. 565.
5. Croucher, Sheila L., *op. cit.*, pp. 36-37.
6. *Ibid.*, p. 38.
7. *Ibid.*
8. Schnapper, Dominique, *Community of Citizens, On the Modern Idea of Nationality,* Transaction Publishers, New Brunswick, New Jersey, 1998, p. 12.
9. *Ibid.*, p. 16.

10. *Ibid.*, p. 24.
11. *Ibid.*, p. 27.
12. Gans, Judith, Citizenship in the Context of Globalization, Working Paper, June 2005, p. 6.
13. *Ibid.*, p. 27.
14. Schnapper, *op. cit.*, 135.
15. Marshall, T.H., *Class, Citizenship and Social Development*, Westport: Greenwood Press, 1973, pp. 65-122.
16. Gunsteren, Herman van, A Theory of Citizenship: Organizing Plurality in Contemporary Democracies, Boulder Colorado: Westview Press, 1998, pp. 13-14.
17. *Ibid.*
18. Lister, R. *Citizenship: Feminist Perspectives,* Basinstoke: Macmillan, 1997, p. 196.
19. Heater, D., *What is Citizenship*, Cambridge, Polity Press, 1999, p. 117.
20. *Ibid.*, p. 121.
21. *Ibid.*, p. 152.
22. Linklater, A. p. 56.
23. Soysal, Y.

3

Class Inequality

The struggle of the disadvantaged for rights as well as improved conditions and especially the rights of citizenship is a prominent thread running through the history of the west. Citizenship has developed not only as a consequence of popular pressure, but also in response to the ruling class's requirements for security, a factor ignored by recent theorists of citizenship. Today citizenship is generally taken to include a universal right to a level of economic and social well being in addition to the rights of equality before the law and political participation.

Modern citizenship, comprising at least universal civil, political and social rights, is not only complex but fraught with internal tensions, as the distinct rights which constitute it tend to generate different and sometimes contradictory pressures. This chapter explains both the relationship between the distinct elements of citizenship and its effects on class inequality.

Historically power has been both concentrated and unitary. Political and economic powers, for instance could be functionally differentiated only as distinct aspects of a single power. In practically all of its instances the human experience has shown that those who posses economic power also control government and law. It is arguably this situation which has provoked and is challenged by the rise of democratic citizenship. The struggle for citizenship has been the struggle against exclusion, and against the inequalities which exclusion produces. But the rise of democratic citizenship has not brought an end to inequality, rather it has produced spheres of equal participation, parallel to those of exclusive power.

The above remarks are unquestionably applicable to a citizenship comprised of civil and political rights. The development of civil citizenship introduced not only equality before the law but also law as an institution free of and formally separated from private property. Indeed, the removal of legal priviledge through citizenship was at the same time the saparation of legal institutions from economic power. The advent of political citizenship similarly provided for political equality, by taking government, or the means of selecting the individuals from which a government could be formed, away from the exclusive control of economic power holders. Thus the advance of citizenship has meant the displacement of exclusion with universal participation, but only in those elements of the erstwhile unitary configuration of power which have been separated from its economic core. It is thus important to remember that while citizenship rights are universal, the principle of citizenship has never been generalized to all social institutions. The economic system in particular and the social classes associated with it remain exclusive in nature and marked by a high degree of inequality and concentration of power. It is on these bases that the capitalist class system can be contrasted with the system of democratic citizenship.

It is pertinent to ask whether social citizenship, which directly addresses the problem of economic equality, has been more successful against economic exclusion than civil and political citizenship.

There can be no doubt that the development of citizenship during the twentieth century has altered the pattern of social inequality. Yet it would be unnecessarily narrow to suggest that citizenship was the only factor in this process. Improvements in the conditions of ordinary people can in many instances be attributed to directly economic causes. The consolidation of the world economy by the 1890's and the international economic competition which accompanied it led employees to improve the conditions of employment for most of their workers in order to raise labour productivity. In addition, new technologies not only destroyed the lowest-paid jobs, and therefore raised the wage floor of inequality, but also formed part of a new situation which enhanced the bargaining of organized labour. The prosperity of the people period from the late 1940's which (until recently) has been responsible for the most optimistic outlooks on the decline of inequality, it also most readily explained in economic terms. Full employment, expanding mass markets and the development of new technologies and their application to production led to rises in living standards which appeared to further reduce the inequalities which appeared to further reduce the inequalities which had more or less been declining since the turn of the century.

T.H. Marshall recognizes that while the first advances

in social rights from the end of the nineteenth century were to make inroads on the pattern of inequality, other forces were at work as well. But the reduction of inequality through economic causes and through citizenship are not unconnected to Marshall. He says that the 'diminution of inequality strengthened the demand for its abolition' and goes on to add that such aspirations have partly been achieved by 'incorporating social rights in the status of citizenship and thus created a universal right to real income which is not appropriate to the market value of the claimant'. Thus Marshall draws citizenship back into the argument in which the decline of inequality can be shown to have a basis in economic developments.

It is in fact crucial to recognize that non-economic sources have influenced the structure of inequality. This is not only to more adequately account for those changes themselves but also to understand the significance of such changes for more general political and social developments. The question immediately arises whether the provision of economic resources as a right of citizenship alters the pattern of inequality but its very basis, and therefore the dynamic and structure of class society.

One possibility is that rights to social goods and services might simply improve the conditions of the disadvantaged without directly dealing with the underlying causes of inequality. Such changes may mitigate the harm economic inequalities cause to individuals by slinging a safety-net of social policy under the disadvantaged. If this is the general outcome of social citizenship, then the principles underlying the operations of the economy and the structure and the process of social class remain untouched by its development. It is possible that under such circumstances social tensions will be reduced and the class antagonism will decline. These things tend not to affect the actual structure of class inequality, however but serve to legitimate it and therefore preserve class priviledge and advantage. Under these circumstances the effect of citizenship on the system of class inequality is primarily political and apologetic.

A quite different possibility is that social citizenship and therefore the provision of economic resources as a right may modify the very principle of economic relationships. Certainly the non-market provision of economic resources would have been inconceivable to the laissez-faire capitalism of the nineteenth century. According to its principles workers separated from the means of material production are compelled to sell their capacity to labour for a wage in order to live. Those unable to derive a livelihood from the labour market in this way had no other access to means of subsistence (except as a dependent wife or child of those in employment.) this harsh and direct relationship between the labour market and income has been modified by social citizenship.It is thus possible to argue that the structure of modern society is subject to a different basis of development than the one which governed laissez-faire capitalism, and therefore that market inequalities no longer determine social differentiation. Bryan Turner, who accepts this view, summarizes it by saying that 'citizenship is an abatement of the class structure of capitalist economic relationships'. Marshall's analysis in 'citizenship and social class' is not clearly directed to either of the positions mentioned here, although his arguments are most readily associated with the second of them. It is important to recognize, however just how tenuous and inconclusive are Marshall's views. Too many readers have ignored the conjectural tone of Marshall's statement that it may be that the inequalities permitted, and even moulded by citizenship do not any longer constitute class distinctions in the sense in which that term is used for past societies. Those same readers have missed the fact that Marshall immediately says that such a question cannot be answered for our ' ignorance on this matter is profound'. What he does insist upon is that 'the preservation of economic inequalities has been made more difficult by the enrichment of the status of citizenship' and also that there are limits inherent in the egalitarian movement.' His conclusion is that 'Class distinctions may survive which have no appropriate economic function, and economic differences which do not correspond with accepted class distinctions' seriously requires interpretation.

In order to assess the impact of the development of citizenship on class inequality it is necessary to identify the changes in the pattern of inequality which are attributable to citizenship rights. When this is done it can be asked in that way such changes affect the nature and operation of the capitalist class system.

The relationship between the expansion of citizenship, especially through the realization of social citizenship, and social and economic inequalities is complex. In principle social citizenship has the effect of encouraging equality of opportunity and is therefore entirely compatible with certain inequalities of condition or outcome. Thus not only might social citizenship reduce some inequalities, but for promoting achievement by merit it may create new ones. Marshall is quite explicit on this point. He says, for Example that the right of the citizen in social selection and mobility is the right to equality of educational opportunity, which has the aim of eliminating hereditary priviledge. The establishment of such a system will initially reveal what Marshall calls 'hidden equalities' for it will permit poor children to show that they are as bright and capable as rich children. 'But the final outcome' he continues is a structure of unequal status fairly apportioned to unequal abilities'. This conclusion is crucial for it demonstrates as Marshall acknowledges that 'citizenship operates as an instrument of social stratification'.

The character of the inequalities created by the practice of citizenship rights is that they are legitimate 'the status acquired by education is carried out into the world bearing the stamp of legitimacy, because it has been conferred by an institution designed to give the citizen has just rights. Elsewhere in 'citizenship and social class' he says that the assumption that the basic equality of citizenship rights is consistent with the inequalities of social class is demonstrated in the fact that 'citizenship has itself become in certain respects, the architect of legitimate social inequality'. It is thus not opposed to inequality as such but to illegitimate inequality, to inequality which cannot be justified on the basis of equal citizenship rights.

In his discussion of the modern class system in which class differences 'emerge from the interplay of a variety of factors related to the institutions of property and education and the structure of the national economy', notes that in such a system social inequality 'provides the incentive to effort and designs the distribution of power'. A feature of such an agreement however is that as the general pattern of inequality does not correspond to an a priority value system which designates the appropriate range of inequality for each level, inequality 'though necessary, may become excessive'. Thus necessary inequality must be distinguished from excessive inequality' from poverty or destitution. Both are part of the capitalist class system; the latter is definitely incompatible with social citizenship and so is the former if it is not legitimate. The basis on which legitimate inequality is necessary under conditions of universal social rights is not clear, for while Marshall says that under these conditions there is a need to preserve differential incomes as a source of economic incentive, he also insists that work ceases to be a market need and becomes instead a duty.He further says that 'in modern democratic society 'Poverty is a disease', but inequality is an essential structural feature'. However the discussion is 'whether the enrichment of citizenship has in fact eradicated poverty but to consider how the system of social class might be altered by the development of citizenship.

Social rights are able to affect the pattern of inequality directly because they permit the provision of benefits in kind which may lead the real income of a citizen to be much greater than their money income. The importance of inequalities formed through market exchanges is seriously reduced when economic values become available outside the market as a universal right of citizenship. This is especially so when these benefits are not only transfer payments but services and resources provided without the intervention of a market exchange but through the state administration of social services. Such developments modify the pattern of inequality directly by reconstituting the distribution of real income and also by altering the significance of the inequalities which remain.

Marshall says that 'the extension of the social services is not primarily a means of equalizing incomes'. He regards this as unimportant, and argues that 'Equalization is not so much between classes as between individuals within a population which is now treated for his purpose as though it were one class. Equality of status is more important than equality of income'.

Social citizenship removes the economic function from inequality and class distinctions by the means of a 'progressive divorce between real and money incomes', as Marshall puts it. Such develcpments have indeed altered the complexion of class relations in removing labour from what Max Weber describes as the 'compulsion of the whip of hunger', which he saw a requirement for the existence of modern capitalism. Through the provision of social security and therefore a real income not based wholly on the receipient's market situation, workers no longer face the choice of employment or starvation, for unemployment no longer means destitution. In this sense citizenship has tempered the power of capitalists in particular and employers in general in their dealings with workers. But it would be difficult to go on from here to argue that social rights have rendered class distinctions economically functionless.

Social security has been important in reducing the risks associated with unemployment for instance, by providing an alternative source of means of subsistence. But the area of personal consumption cannot be full locus of class experience any more than it can be the entire substance of economic inequality, as Marshall's argument implies.

Persons who possess property (including the family house) enjoy a number of advantages over those who do not. Perhaps the most pervasive economic function of wealth is its role in borrowing money. As funds are generally loaned against existing assests wealth permits property owners to spend in excess of their current income. This means that the tendency for social citizenship to narrow the range of the distribution of real income is counteracted by the borrowing capacity of the wealthy , which widens it. Inequalities of wealth are not rendered economically functionless by the incorpcration of social rights in citizenship. On the contrary, wealth continues to be the principal determinant of economic well-being inspite of the provision of benefits which might increase the real income of social citizens.

The identity of class divisions with social perpetual or cultural differences, which is explicit in Marshall's conception of class, indicates a seriously inadequate treatment of the problem. Class contains a cultural element certainly. But social classes cannot exist as discrete entities; and social class cannot be defined by the conception held by its members of their relations with others. Any difference between the cultures of different classes will largely derive from the Assymetrical relations between classes qua classes. That classes are superordinate or subordinate, dominating or subject to domination. Is ultimately responsible for the different social perceptions and relations of the persons within them. Unless this fact is included in the definition we are not dealing with classes but merely with culturally defined groups. The relations between social classes are prior to the relations within them, and inter class relations are determined by such things as the power of private property in the means of production, mentioned above, which is not 'strung out on a continuous scale' but yields a clear division between those who do and those who do not possess it.

Common experiences across the divisions of social inequality may mediate the cultural boundaries which separate social classes. Such a development will not reduce the distance between classes, although it may permit individuals to feel that the differences between them which remain should be regarded as less important than what they have come to share through the development of a common social citizenship. These things do not indicate a 'class fusion' as Marshall supposes, for the basis of class differences in the relations of domination and subordination are untouched by the harmonizing social perceptions which he hypothesizes will emerge with social citizenship. Indeed the changes in the 'qualitative aspects of social differentiation' which Marshall describes as resulting from the universalization of social services will be highly unstable if the class relations he ignores remain unchanged. The equalization of persons as citizens might affect the social perception of social differences but it cannot modify the material relations between the classes. In other words the development of citizenship rights may change the way in which people identify themselves and it may alter their feelings about social and class inequalities.

Patters of inequality or stratification may be modified by developments in citizenship rights, although it is necessary to recognize that other forces are also at work in this process. The class structure, however cannot be changed by universal social rights, which treat only distributional arrangements and ignore the institutions of economic and social power which preserve class domination and exploitation. Rather than alter the class structure citizenship tends to legitimate it by contributing to a decline of class identity and resentment It should be noted that the provision of equal citizenship rights may promote an awareness of the great inequalities of economic advantage which such rights themselves cannot remove and therefore encourage inter-class comparisons which promote class resentment and conflict.

Citizenship and class are based on opposing principles, as Marshall says, one on equality and freedom the other on inequality and domination. But the things to which the equality of citizenship refer are not the same as these which make up class inequality. It is for this reason that citizenship and social class can continue to exist together. If their co-existence is sometimes full of tension it is not because of any logical incompatibility between them, but is rather a result of the endeavors of socially subordinate groups to overcome their disadvantages and lay claim to rights which may not be realized in an unequal society.

4

Women and Citizenship

Introduction

There is no gender but only women, men and genders constructed through particular historical struggles ... over which races, classes, ... sexes etc ... will have access to resources and power[1].

This quotation describes that gender is a socially constructed concept that affects the way both men and women behave and think. A poststructuralist perspective aims to look beneath the surface of what men and women say, in order to reveal how discourses and relations of power influence our lives. This means revealing that which is not obvious in the way we speak, write, interact or even make decisions about our lives. Our socio-cultural, political and individual histories inevitably contribute to the meanings we give to ourselves, our societal roles and our relationships with others.

Feminist critiques of the concept of citizenship (as both a social and legal status) have argued that it is distinctly male and predicated on an idealist notion of the white, European, middle class, able bodied man. Indeed, most countries can reveal histories that demonstrate the open oppression or denial of women's access to public slife and this applies, of course, to other social groups such as migrants or people with disabilities. To emphasise these historical origins of citizenship values, English historical texts are cited as portraying citizenship as a man's duty while women's lives were rendered invisible.[2] Even the words and descriptions associated with the active citizenship were more closely associated with stereotypical masculine characteristics such as impartial, dispassionate and unemotional behaviour, defending one's country. Words associated with femininity such as nurturing, caring and emotion are not seen as valued qualities in the active citizen.[3]

Feminist poststructuralist or pluralistic perspectives argue that citizenship activities should be interpreted more broadly. There are a number of dimensions that influence this requirement. They include the notions of *independence*—a valued citizenship quality—and *interdependence*—a more relational way of viewing citizen connectedness;[4] the *vocabulary* (and its implied meanings) that is associated with active citizenship; the concept of family as a private domain that is ignored for its contribution to citizenship;[5] and the need to recognise that *women's issues* should be given equal prominence in democratic structures and political decision making. Lister argues that political activities should be defined more broadly so that 'society' includes 'family'—where many of women's activities are often located. Furthermore, for many women, their political activity is through neighbourhood action. Yet their activities often fail to be located in formal democratic structures that would enable their issues to be taken forward. In other words, it is argued, we need a multi-layered concept of citizenship with a 'broader understanding of the significance of difference'[6]. By highlighting social, rather than civil, citizenship we enhance the moral relationship between citizens which requires involving more women actively in the formal political process. Prokhovnik argues that citizenship should be seen as a broader concept than its political or socio-economic concerns.[7] This would also create space for new definitions of masculinities so that men, too, are encouraged to deconstruct their own gendered practices.

As today's theory of equality laments on that stark differences no longer prevail, this chapter reveals more subtle evidence of gender disparities in the way men and women learned to be, and behaved as, active citizens. Not all country researchers felt the differences were equally significant, especially amongst the younger generation, but in most cases there was acknowledgement of attitudinal trends trend that still encouraged these disparities.

Accordingly, Citizenship, is learned differently by different social groups to their assumed status in society and according to how policy decisions privilege certain qualities of the good citizen above others. Even where women are not constrained by family commitments, their role and status within society may already be internalised and embedded in social structures that define men and women normatively according to their gender. Formal education, and informal learning, have their part to play in challenging normative values and raising awareness of issues to do with power relations, oppression and hegemony. The core theories of dependence/interdependency; family/private space and rights/responsibilities may be an important focal point for effective education and learning for gender sensitive active citizenship.

Porter, amongst others argues that interdependence (rather than the more separate notion of independence) should be taught as a feature of responsible citizenship[8]. This would highlight 'the ways that independence requires dependency and nurturance in our intimate lives and results in the connectedness of citizens in our socio-political lives' In other words we need a more inclusive recognition of our relationship to one another and our collective responsibilities towards society. 'Caring' is not just a private, female activity. It is part of the interdependency of family upbringing for citizenship responsibility. A recognition of the concept of interdependency would then lead to a broader recognition of the link between the public and private worlds of citizenship and the increasing role that all individuals play in both. There are a number of feminist arguments around this issue. Prokhovnik argues that re-defining the public private distinction is an ethical issue. It means recognising citizenship practice in the private realm as part of a diversity of citizenship practices that are already undertaken by both men and women:

> It is not that women need to be liberated from the private realm, in order to take part in the public realm as equal citizens, but that women—and men—already undertake responsibilities of citizenship in both the public and private realms.[9]

Yuval Davis suggests that recognising the private

(family) sphere as contributing to the state and civil domains of citizenship activity will influence the systems of welfare, power and political organisation.[10] Otherwise, even where women have received state support for domestic commitments, the loci of control in public spaces are still with men. She goes further to point out that being an active citizen must include different definitions for what counts as active. For instance, disabled people cannot carry out normative citizen duties if they are defined by such criteria as the ability to die for your country.

Flax proposes that even the discourse of 'equality' needs to change, so that new meanings can be introduced.[11] She proposes that 'justice'[12] is a more appropriate word since it signifies the need to question and analyse relationships and behaviours that have created power imbalances. It also implies the need for fundamental review of normative behaviours.

This feminist, ethical dimension gives greater significance to marginalised experiences. By highlighting social, rather than civil citizenship we enhance the moral relationship between citizens. This includes involving more women actively in the formal political process as well as recognising the conditions necessary to support care responsibilities in the process.

The understanding of these arguments for an effective education and learning for active citizenship lie in the need to learn new values, identities and expectations. Whilst critical education can help women find new ways of representing themselves it also requires a fundamental change of learning across society—so that men and women learn how to value women and other marginalised groups differently. This brings us back to the analytical question of power. In other words, how do people act as conscious subjects towards each other and what is their understanding of ethical responsibility? Of course, for such analysis to be effective we first have to recognise there is still a gender problem. Secondly we have to be prepared to examine our own responsibility towards the problem. Then we have to be prepared to act differently, to re-learn new ways of seeing ourselves (our subjectivities) and new ways of relating.

Women, Nationality and Citizenship

Nationality signifies the legal relationship between an individual and a State. It not only provides individuals with a sense of belonging and security, but also creates a legal link between the individual and her State. Nationals are entitled to the protection of their

State—which is of increasing significance in the globalizing world with its large-scale movements of people. International law makes clear that a State may provide its protection to a national who has suffered an international wrong while abroad. Thus, a State is entitled to provide its nationals abroad with consular assistance, and make a diplomatic claim for harm caused to its nationals which constitutes violations of international law. A State has a duty, in international law, to admit its nationals and allow them to reside in its territory. The unqualified right to hold the passport of the State is also a function of nationality. In many cases, nationality is the legal basis for the exercise of citizenship. Although frequently used interchangeably with nationality, the term citizenship has a wider meaning, and denotes a status bestowed on full members of a community. In many countries, the full exercise of civil, political, economic, social and cultural rights is predicated on nationality. Nationality frequently determines whether individuals are entitled to participate fully in the political process, including through voting, and to exercise the right to work, the right to education and the right to health. The right to own land may also be contingent on nationality. It may also determine whether individuals may hold public office, or have access to the judicial system or public services, such as legal aid. As the Committee on the Elimination of Discrimination against Women noted in its General Recommendation on Equality in Marriage and Family Relations, "nationality is critical to full participation in society". Those who lack the nationality of the State in which they reside are regarded as aliens. Aliens may incur a range of legal consequences which have practical and personal disadvantages. The right of non-nationals to reside in the State in which they live is not absolute, but conditional. Non-nationals may also have limited access to the full range of citizenship rights. They may be denied the right to vote and to exercise other aspects of the right to political participation.

They may have limited access to public office or the judicial system.

Their enjoyment of the rights to work, freedom of movement or the full range of education, health, housing and social security rights and benefits may be more limited than that of nationals. Bestowal of nationality is an attribute of State sovereignty and, within some constraints imposed by international law, each State is entitled to lay down its own rules governing the grant of its nationality, with the International Court of Justice stating in 1955 that "international law leaves it to each State to lay down the rules governing the grant of its own nationality". Nationality laws are rarely simple or comprehensive, and their technical nature makes them inaccessible to many people. Moreover, movements of peoples across international borders frequently make the laws of more than one State applicable in the determination of a person's nationality. Inconsistency between, and lack of coordination of, nationality laws between and among States means that nationality may be uncertain or contested, causing hardship to the individuals concerned. The determination of its nationals defines the State's self-identification, for example, as a homogeneous political entity, or as a State committed to multiculturalism. Ethnic conflicts over the last decade have demonstrated the violence,regional instability and personal insecurity that can be generated by claims for independent statehood defined by nationality in some sub-State entities. Sovereign States closely guard their right under international law to determine the construction of their populations through their nationality laws, as well as through laws and policies on immigration which are closely connected to nationality laws.

Married Women's Dependent Nationality

Historically, many States adopted the patriarchal position that a woman's legal status is acquired through her relationship to a man—first her father and then her husband. Although the laws of most States provide that nationality is conferred through birth or descent, or a combination of these, a widely accepted principle—law in most States at the beginning of the twentieth century was that of dependent nationality,or the unity of nationality of spouses. The result of the application of this principle was that a woman who married a foreigner automatically acquired the nationality of her husband upon marriage. Usually this was accompanied by the loss of her own nationality. The rationale for the principle of dependent nationality derived from two assumptions: first, that all members of a family should have the same nationality and, secondly, that important decisions affecting the family would be made by the husband.

The assumption that all members of a family should have the same nationality was based on the view that nationality entailed loyalty to one's State of nationality. It was believed that if a married woman were to have a nationality different from that of her husband, her loyalties would be divided, and she might be placed in a conflictual and intolerable situation. This assumption was also linked to the idea of citizenship, which relates to a person's public identity: the relationship between an individual and the State. Loyalty to the State is the counterpart of the State's duty to protect its citizens. In many States, the assumption that a married woman's primary location is in the private sphere, within the home, and under the protection of her husband, has prevailed.

Accordingly, her need for a separate public identity and legal relationship with a State is not taken into account. In States where one of the primary obligations of citizenship is military service, a male definition of citizenship is reinforced. In an international order in which conflict between States was deemed inevitable, permitting spouses to maintain separate nationalities was regarded as unacceptable since conflict between the couple's different States would cause divided loyalties within the household. Potential for familial disruption on these grounds was resolved in favour of family unity, with the wife being required to assume her husband's nationality. Allowing her to hold dual nationality, predicating that loyalty was owed by her to her State of nationality, as well as that of her husband, was not regarded as a viable option. Where the assumption that important family decisions would be made by the husband was concerned, the prevailing view was that the choice of the couple's place of abode would be made by the husband. Generally, this would be in his State of nationality.

Laws that entrench the principle of dependent nationality disempower married women by depriving them of any choice about their nationality. As such, these laws, and married women's nationality in general, have long attracted the attention of feminist activists. They were among one of the first issues that women sought to place on the international legal agenda, alongside other issues of social and political inequality affecting women, including the right to vote.

The creation of the United Nations provided another forum in which to address the issue of women's nationality. The United Nations commission on the Status of Women, established in 1946 to prepare recommendations and reports to the Economic and Social Council on promoting women's rights in political, economic, civil and educational fields and to make recommendations on urgent problems requiring immediate attention in the field of human rights, identified this area as one of its priority concerns. Responses to the annual Questionnaire on the Legal

Status and Treatment of Women circulated by the Commission revealed that in most countries laws were based on the principle of dependent nationality and the assumption that married women would automatically take their husband's nationality.

Contemporary international law approaches gender-based discrimination in nationality laws in two ways. The first addresses the situation where spouses have different nationalities by entitling a married woman to retain her nationality irrespective of the nationality of her husband. It also seeks to facilitate the acquisition by both spouses of the other spouse's nationality through requirements which are more flexible than for others applying for naturalization.

The second seeks to minimize the legal consequences of lack of nationality by attempting to reduce the incidence of statelessness and guaranteeing human rights protections to all persons within a State's jurisdiction, regardless of their nationality. As will be seen, neither approach is comprehensive, and there are problems with both the scope of legal protection provided and implementation.

Supranational Citizenship

Another model, also from Europe, attaches citizenship to a supranational entity, in this case the European Union. The vision is based on the identification of a person as European, as well as a national of an individual State. Article 8 of the Treaty of European Union (Maastricht Treaty), 1992, provides that nationals of the individual States of the Union are citizens of the Union. At present, the attributes of European citizenship are limited to the right to move freely and reside within any State of the Union; the right when outside the Union to seek diplomatic protection from the authorities of any member State; and the right to petition the European Parliament and to apply to the European Ombudsman. The concept of European citizenship is not detached from that of national citizenship, as such citizenship is accorded only to the nationals of member States of the Union. The sovereignty of member States with respect to nationality laws is therefore not weakened; and European citizenship heightens the exclusion for those who are denied nationality in any State of the Union, including migrant workers and, in some instances, their children.

Article 4 (*d*): Neither marriage nor the dissolution of a marriage between a national of a State Party and an alien, nor the change of nationality by one of the spouses during marriage, shall automatically affect the nationality of the other spouse.

Article 5: Non-discrimination

(1) The rules of a State Party on nationality shall not contain distinctions or include any practice which amounts to discrimination on the grounds of sex, religion, race, colour, or national or ethnic origin.

(2) Each State Party shall be guided by the principle of non-discrimination between its nationals, whether they are nationals by birth or have acquired its nationality subsequently.[14]

The passage and implementation of legislation at the national level will not by itself guarantee equality between women and men in the conferment and enjoyment of nationality and citizenship rights, but the existence of such laws is essential. Discriminatory nationality laws create vulnerability for women. This vulnerability has great practical impact at a time when huge numbers of women are leaving their own States, voluntarily through migration and involuntarily (through displacement and trafficking). Susceptibility to violence, exploitation and loss of access to children who hold a different nationality is increased when women are denied the protections accorded to citizens and nationals. Unlike many other violations of women's human rights, the denial of nationality to women or their children on an equal basis with men involves no non-State actor.

Feminist Critique of Citizenship

Feminist theorists such as Mouffe[15], Yuval-Davis[16], Lister and Fraser have attempted to resolve some of the critiques of citizenship generated in the previous section. They have come up with ways of reformulating the public/private divide that marginalizes women, including those excluded from citizenship rights and participation, and have defined ways in which women can become agents and political actors. The following two sections show how reworking citizenship from a gender perspective has influenced and been influenced by activists and development actors. They illustrate citizenship as inclusion and practice at the economic level (economic equality), the cultural level (norms and values) and the personal level (family and domestic life).[17] They explore activities by social movements, women's groups, donors and national and international political bodies.

Participation can range from the local, through the national and regional to engagement in the international political arena[18]. National policy is often the most effective arena for promoting gender equality and women's citizenship rights. However, it is engagement in local struggles that is particularly significant for most women, given their lack of experience in formal politics, their family commitments and restrictions on their mobility. These lead to recommendations which will be drawn together in the final section.

The Public/Private Divide: A Challenge

Because the exclusion of women is based on a particular understanding of the public/private divide, including women requires a redefinition of both private and public arenas. Conventional ideas that women's place is in the private or domestic sphere leads to their exclusion from formal politics, from rights, and from acknowledgement of their contribution to society. It can also mean that women's informal associations are defined as non-political social groups or service providers.

Challenging the public/private divide means identifying "personal" oppressions that occur in the private or domestic sphere, in sexuality, reproduction and family life, as structural and widespread issues which can be dealt with in the language of citizenship rights. As such this "puts in" a range of activities and identities that are left out of citizenship rights and expands the capacity of individuals to shape both the intimate and the broader decisions that affect their lives. In citizenship struggles over the past two decades this has primarily relied on the efforts of women's rights activists pushing for better legislation and policies to protect women from violence, particularly domestic violence, as their citizenship right.

Political participation is often only seen as that which occurs within state or governmental arenas and, to a lesser extent, in civil society activist groups. Many feminists have pointed out that politics is about the ability to have an input into decisions at all levels through mobilising support from those around you.

Many women who do not, or are not able to participate in formal structures, do participate in informal networks and forms of decision-making. Researching these activities and valuing their work makes it clear that women are political beings and that women's interests are the stuff of politics. They also extend the spaces within which citizenship can take place – from narrow views that citizenship participation is about voting or standing for elections to a wider view that recognises community-level and informal actions. This wider view can strengthen the political potential of women's organisations and encourage institutions to see them as valuable sources of information and input into policy.

Challenging Exclusion from Citizenship Rights on the Basis of Gender

Since a key problem with citizenship is exclusion on the basis of power and social roles, much thinking has gone into how to include the excluded. Reframing feminist concerns in the language of inclusion in rights and participation may help to make women and their concerns more integral to development thought and practice.

A key concern of feminists has been to find ways of taking gender and other differences into account through expanding citizen rights based on their needs.

People can draw on the emancipatory potential of universal principles such as equality, while demanding equity in their diversities. Gender analysis can create better understanding of the different activities, responsibilities, interests and priorities of men and women.[19]

Recognising difference means moving away from universal, homogeneous ideas of women and women's interests to bring in the real experiences of women. Often the needs of the less powerful in a society are not articulated and ways need to be found to bring out voices that are usually silent. This means involving marginalised groups in defining their needs and ensuring that development institutions make the necessary shifts in their cultures, procedures and practices so as to be responsive to marginalized groups including women.

Mobilising for Change – Promoting active Gendered Citizenship

The right to have a right, to politicise needs, to have influence over wider decision-making processes that affect one's life, and the right to act, are fundamental to the project of equality in development.[20] Much thought has gone into questions of how to enable oppressed groups to take up their citizenship rights to participation in decision-making, as a prerequisite to other rights.[21] Constructing more inclusive forms of citizenship entails processes of change that go beyond policy analysis to include social movements and the politics of everyday life as seen in community-level struggles. Bringing these ideas to development offers a way of involving the poor and marginalised, including women, in holding institutions accountable.[22]

The Beijing Platform for Action was formulated at the 4th World Conference on Women in 1995 and subsequently adopted by 189 countries. Beijing served as the basis of NGO and activism by women's movements in many parts of the world. It ushered in a new era of transnational feminist networking that was one of the key factors in promoting institutional change and moves towards gender mainstreaming in development and other policy arenas.[23] This international mobilisation has linked in with national and community-level struggles that draw on international instruments to push governments to be more responsive to women's interests.

Raising Awareness

Gender-based exclusion, like other forms of exclusion, works by co-opting the excluded into seeing their exclusion as natural " as if there were no alternative. In many cases women's autonomy is constrained by male authority and the demands on their time given the unequal gendered division of labour. It is important to note that women can and do overcome these constraints and that it is possible to be a subject of subordination while at the same time acting to improve situations of poverty and inequality.

A first step is for people to become aware that their exclusion is an injustice and that things can change. In turn, taking up actions and winning demands reinforces the idea that change is possible and struggling is worthwhile.

Conclusion

From this brief understanding with some women's experiences we can see that the concept of active citizenship is subjectively defined according to normative values at a given point in time and place. How people learn the formalities of active citizenship may be similar across most sectors of European society. The learning of citizenship entitlement, however, is defined both formally and informally through normalised value systems and social expectations for different social groups. Women, men, and other social groups learn to act out roles which may or may not be understood in public documents as active citizenship. Their understanding of their rights and responsibilities in relation to others will be learned, at least in part, according to how they are positioned in society. The social structures of society will also either facilitate or hinder their interactions with political decision making.[24]

To promote a more pluralistic, ethical citizenship, we will need to understand how societal systems, structures and practices contribute to hegemonic practices or how they may enable new possibilities for agency's self determination. The concept of being a woman interfaced with race, disability or class has the potential to displace her potential public role in society because her perceived gender status is made more visible than her personal qualities. Even today, women's relationship to men is often still defined by their gender and family position. So there is still work to be done. For instance, policy and educational practices can explore how women are socially constructed formally and informally. An ethical citizenship education would examine how much women's visibility enables a shared power relationship with men. Education for active citizenship, then, depends in part on how people are taught to be regarded in society. Formal and informal educational situations determine which skills are valued and which are not. So it is up to us, as individuals and members of wider society, to publicly value the interconnectedness of work, family, the state and civil society in helping to create tomorrow's citizens.[25]

This chapter has shown how feminist theory and activism have re-framed citizenship by challenging the public/private divide, including those excluded from politics and society, and by promoting active engagement with institutions. This work has been seen and encouraged by gender and development practitioners and policy makers. Rethinking development along the lines of citizenship rights and participation is a new and exciting area of theory and practice in mainstream development. However, rights and participation that do not acknowledge gender as an important relationship of unequal power will remain incomplete and exclusionary.

How we think about or define situations has a direct bearing on what we think must be done to rectify them. Gendered citizenship can explain why gender equality is central to all development goals. It can be instrumental in mobilising allies and developing a shared vision on gender concerns within development institutions.[26] For those working both "inside" and "outside" institutions it can provide a rationale and a strategy for addressing discrimination and exclusion.

Gendered citizenship in practice can suggest solutions through a wide range of measures from legal reform of women's rights to gender mainstreaming in policy; from better, gendered needs assessments to education and awareness-raising amongst the general public. Above all, such measures must be geared towards combating the social and political exclusion of women and others marginalised on the basis of gender.

Citizenship is not just about a position inside or outside society. It also implies action – participation in the life, development and decisions of the community. The shifts in meanings and practice of citizenship along the lines outlined above imply an improved and more dynamic interaction between people, citizens' organisations and governance institutions. Activism promoting the interests of marginalised groups such as women has for many years challenged unequal and oppressive power relations that limit rights to full citizenship. Mobilising in civil society demonstrates the involvement of groups in decisions that affect their lives and the lives of others in their communities. Social movements, activists and other civil society.

QUESTIONS

1. Explain why women and citizenship rights have always been a ground for debates?
2. Women, citizenship and nationalities are always been contested terms. Explain how?
3. Can citizenship rights become more inclusive with gender mainstreaming?

NOTES

1. Harding, 1991, p. 151.
2. Brindle and Arnot, 1999.
3. Sawer, 1996.
4. Porter, 2001 and Lister 1997.

5. Yuval Davis, 1997.
6. Lister 1997, p. 197.
7. Proknovnik, 1998.
8. Porter, 2001, p. 5.
9. Proknovnik, 1998, p. 84.
10. Yuval Davis, 1997.
11. Flax, 1992.
12. *Ibid.*, p. 194.
13. European Community Treaty, article 8:(1) Citizenship of the Union is hereby established. Every person holding the nationality of a member State shall be a citizen of the Union. The concept of European citizenship was expanded further by the Amsterdam Treaty, in force 3 May 1999, adding paragraphs a-e to article 8 or the Maastrich Treaty.
14. The Committee on the Elimination of Racial Discrimination has considered a number of situations where the rights of non-nationals are more limited than those of nationals. (United Nations doc CERD/C/54/D/8/1996). The preliminary report of the Special Rapporteur on the rights of non-citizens indicates that in a number of countries constitutional guarantees of human rights apply only to nationals (E/CN.4/Sub.2/2001020/Add.1).
15. Mouffe, C., 1992.
16. Fraser, N. 2000.
17. Sen, G. 2003.
18. Kabeer, N. 1994.
19. United Nations Office of the Special Adviser on Gender Issues and Advancement of Women (UN OSAGI), 2002, Gender Mainstreaming: An Overview, report, New York: United Nations.
20. Mukhopadhyay, M., (ed.) 2003.
21. Mouffe, C. 1992.
22. Jones, E. and Gaventa, J., 2002.
23. True, J. and Mintrom, M. 2001.
24. Preece, J. and Edinsingha, P., 2001, p. 45.
25. *Ibid.*, p. 45.
26. Hunt, J., 2004.

REFERENCES

Basten, F. and van der Veen, R.,: Life histories of active citizens in the Netherlands, in: Snick A, Stroobants, V. and Wildermeersch, D. (eds) *Learning citizenship and governance in Europe: Overall review and analysis – analysis of life histories,* Unit of Social Pedagogy, Catholic University of Leuven, Belgium, 2001, pp. 116-148.

Brindle, P., Arnot, M.,: England expects every man to do his duty: the gendering of the citizenship textbook 1940-1966, *Oxford Review of Education,* volume 25 numbers 1&2, 1999, pp. 103-123.

Centre for Social and Educational Research (CREA): Life histories horizontal analysis – Spain, in: Snick A., Stroobants, V. and Wildermeersch, D. (eds) *Learning citizenship and governance in Europe: Overall review and analysis – analysis of life histories,* Unit of Social Pedagogy, Catholic University of Leuven, Belgium, 2002, pp. 186-213.

Edith Brown Weiss, (ed.) *Environmental Change and International Law—New Challenges and Dimensions,* United Nations University Press, 1992.

Flax, J.,: Beyond equity: gender, justice and difference, in: Bock, G., James, S. (eds), *Beyond Equality and Difference: Citizenship, Feminist Politics Feminist Subjectivity,* Routledge: London, 1992, pp. 178-193.

Harding, S.,: *Whose science? Whose knowledge? Thinking from women's lives,* Open University Press: Milton Keynes, 1991, 319 pp.

Hobson, B.,: Economic citizenship: reflections through the European Union Policy Mirror, in: Hobson, B. (ed.), *Gender and Citizenship in Transition,* Routledge: New York, 2000, pp. 84-117.

Jones, A.,: Teaching post-structuralist feminist theory in education: student resistances, *Gender and Education*, volume 9, number 3, 1997, pp. 261-269.

Lister, R.,: *Citizenship: Feminist Perspectives*, Macmillan: Basingstoke, 1997, 284 pp.

Yuval Davis, N.,: *Gender and Nation*, Sage: London, 1997, 157 pp.

Porter, E.,: Interdependence, parenting and responsible citizenship, *Journal of Gender Studies*, volume 10, number 1, 2001, pp. 5-15.

Sawer, M.,: Gender, metaphor and the state, *Feminist Review*, volume 5, 1996, pp. 118-134.

Podemenik, D., Ivancic, A., Novak, D. and Mohorcic Spolar, V.,: Learning active citizenship and governance in Slovenia, in: Snick A, Stroobants, V. and Wildermeersch, D. (eds) Learning citizenship and governance in Europe: Overall review and analysis – analysis of life histories, Unit of Social Pedagogy, Catholic University of Leuven, Belgium, 2001, pp. 149-185.

Preece, J.: Feminist perspectives on the learning of citizenship and governance, *Compare*, volume 32, 2002, pp. 21-33.

Preece, J. and Edirisingha, P.,: Learning to be an active citizen: a gender perspective, *Sociale Interventie*, volume 4, 2001, pp. 37-46.

Prokhovnik, R.,: Public and private citizenship: from gender invisibility to feminist inclusiveness, *Feminist Review*, volume 60, 1998, pp. 84-104.

Siim, B., (2000): *Gender and citizenship: politics and agency in France, Britain and Denmark*, Cambridge University Press: Cambridge, 2000, 220 pp.

T. H. Marshall, *Class, Citizenshipand Social Development* (New York, Doubleday,), 1965, p. 92; Nitza Berkovitch, *From Motherhood to Citizenship: Women's Rights and International Organizations* (Baltimore, Johns Hopkins University Press, 1999), pp. 10-15.

Official Records of the General Assembly, Forty-ninth Session (A/49/38), report of the Committee on the Elimination of Discrimination against Women on its thirteenth session, 1994, p. 2.

The Committee on the Elimination of Racial Discrimination has considered a number of situations where the rights of non-nationals are more limited than those of nationals. (United Nations doc. CERD/C/54/D/8/1996). The preliminary report of the Special Rapporteur on the rights of non-citizens indicates that in a number of countries constitutional guarantees of human rights apply only to nationals (E/CN.4/Sub.2/2001/20/Add.1).

Economic and Social Council resolution 11 (II) of 21 June 1946 established the Commission on the Status of Women. International Covenant on Civil and Political Rights, General Assembly resolution 2200 A (XXI), United Nations doc. A/63/6 (1966). Convention on the Rights of the Child, General Assembly resolution 44/25 (1989), annex, United Nations doc. A/44/49 (1989).

European Community Treaty, article 8: (1) Citizenship of the Union is hereby established. Every person holding the nationality of a member State shall be a citizen of the Union. The concept of European citizenship was expanded further by the Amsterdam Treaty, in force 1 May 1999, adding paragraphs a-e to article 8 of the Maastricht Treaty.

Bell, E., 'Gender and PRSPs: with experiences from Tanzania, Bolivia, Viet Nam and Mozambique', *BRIDGE Report* 67, Brighton: Institute of Development Studies, 2003.

Bissio, R., 'Civil Society and the MDGs', *Development Policy Journal,* 2003, 3: 151-160.

Bulbeck, C., *Re-Orienting Western Feminisms: Women's Diversity in a Postcolonial World,* Cambridge: Cambridge University Press, 1998.

Butto, Zarzar, A., 'Gender and the Participatory Budget in Recife', *Gender and Development In Brief* 12, Brighton: Institute of Development Studies, 2003.

Chambers, R. and Blackburn J., 'PRA " The Power of Participation', *IDS Policy Briefing* 7, Brighton: Institute of Development Studies, 1996.

Clulow, M., 'Gender Equity and Local Governance: A Study of the San Salvador Municipal Gender Equity Policy', London: One World Action, 2003.

Cortez Ruiz, C., 'Rights and Citizenship among Indigenous Women: Struggles, Hopes and Fears in Chiapas', in N. Kabeer (ed.), *Meanings and Expressions of Citizenship: Perspectives from the North and South,* London: Zed Books, 2004.

Cross C, and Friedman M., 'Women and tenure: marginality and the left hand power' in Meer S. (ed.), *Women, Land and Authority: Perspectives from South Africa,* Cape Town: David Philip in association with National Land Committee, 1997.

Deere, C.D., 'Women's Land Rights and Rural Social Movements in the Brazilian Agrarian Reform', *Journal of Agrarian Change,* Vol. 3, No. 1 and 2, January and April 2003: 257-288.

Dominguez, E., 2001, 'Citizenship and Women in Mexico', in N. Kabeer (ed.), *Discussing women's empowerment: theory and practice*, Stockholm: Sida: 88"113.

E°im, S., 'Impact of Government Budgets on Poverty and Gender Equality', paper presented to the Inter-Agency Workshop on Improving the Effectiveness of Integrating Gender into Government Budgets, London, Commonwealth Secretariat, April 26–7, 2000.

Fraser, N., 'Rethinking Recognition', *New Left Review* 3, May/June, 2000.

Hofbauer Balmori, 'Gender and Budgets', BRIDGE *Cutting Edge Pack*, Brighton: Institute of Development Studies, 2003.

Hunt, J., 'Successful Strategies for Addressing Gender Equality Issues in Programs and Projects: What Works', *Development Bulletin*, Australian Development Studies Network, 2004.

International Development Association and International Monetary Fund, 2002, 'Review of the Poverty Reduction Strategy Paper (PRSP) Approach: Main Findings', Approved by the Staffs of the World Bank and the IMF. http://www.worldbank.org/poverty/strategies/review/findings.pdf

Jones, E. and Gaventa, J., 'Concepts of Citizenship: A Review', *Development Bibliography* 1, Brighton: Institute of Development Studies, 2002.

Kabeer, N., 'Citizenship and the boundaries of the acknowledged community: identity, affiliation and exclusion', *IDS Working Paper* 171, Brighton: Institute of Development Studies, 2002.

——, *Reversed realities: gender hierarchies in development thought*, London: Verso, 1994.

Kraft, D., 2003, 'The Changing Role of Africa's Women', Independent Online (IOL), December 11, 2003 http://www.iol.co.za/index.php?click_id=68&art_id=qw107111754327B213&set_id=148

Lawson, V., 'Gender Mainstreaming NGOs in Africa: An Emerging Agenda of the Globalisation Era', paper, Atakpamé: Extended Agricultural Group, 2003.

Lister, R., 'Justice Equality and Dependency: a critical social policy perspective', paper presented at Symposium on Nancy Fraser's work, Warwick, 22 March. http://www.warwick.ac.uk/fac/soc/sociоogy/gender/events/symposium/lister, 2003a.

——, 'Feminist Theory and Practice of Citizenship', paper presented at annual conference of DVPW (German Political Science Association), Mainz, September http://www.dvpw.de/data/doc/ad-hocCitizen.pdf, 2003b.

——, 'Citizenship and Gender' in K.Nash and A. Scott (eds), *Blackwell Companion to Political Sociology*, Oxford: Blackwell, 2001.

——, 'Citizenship: Towards a Feminist Synthesis', *Feminist Review*, 57: 28-48, 1997.

Macdonald, M., 'Gender Equality and Mainstreaming in the policy and practice of the UK Department for International Development', a briefing from the UK Gender and Development (GAD) Network, London: GAD Network, 2003.

Machreq/Maghreb Gender Linking and Information Project, 2003, 'Gender, Citizenship and Nationality', draft reportBeirut: Mac/Mag GLIP.

Mamdani, M., *Citizen and Subject: Contemporary Africa and the Legacy of Late Colonialism*, Princeton: Princeton University Press, 1996.

Mouffe, C., 'Feminism, Citizenship and Radical Democratic Politics' in J. Butler and J.W. Scott (eds), *Feminists Theorise the Political*, London and New York: Routledge, 1992.

Mukhopadhyay, M., (ed.), *Governing for Equity: Gender Citizenship and Governance*, Amsterdam: Royal Tropical Institute, 2003.

Mukhopadhyay, M., Meer, S. and Appel, M., 'Creating Voice, Carving Space: Defining Good Governance from a Gender Perspective', final research report, Gender, Citizenship and Governance Programme, Amsterdam: Royal Tropical Institute, 2003.

Norris, P., *Democratic Phoenix: Reinventing Political Activism*, New York: Cambridge University Press, 2002.

Nzomo, M., 'From OAU to AU and NEPAD: Regional integration processes in Africa and African women', keynote address made at Regional Strategy Meeting on Women's Political Participation and Gender Mainstreaming in AU and NEPAD, Nairobi, 27"31 October. http://www.sarpn.org.za/documents/d0000608/page1.php, 2003.

Philips A., *Democracy and Difference*, Oxford: Blackwell Publishers, 1993.

Sen, G., 'Feminist Politics in a Fundamentalist World', in M. Mukhopadhyay (ed.), *Governing for Equity: Gender Citizenship and Governance*, Amsterdam: Royal Tropical Institute, 2003.

Sen, G. and Grown, C., *Development Crisis and Alternative Visions: Third World Women's Perspectives*, New York: Monthly Review Press, 1985.

Shabbir Cheema, G., Preface, 'Women's Political Participation and Good Governance: 21st Century

Challenges', report, New York: UNDP. http://magnet.undp.org/new/pdf/gender/wpp/women_book.pdf, 2000.

True, J. and Mintrom, M., 'Transnational Networks and Policy Diffusion: The Case of Gender Mainstreaming', *International Studies Quarterly,* 2001, 45: 25-57.

United Nations Development Programme (UNDP), 'Women's Political Participation and Good Governance: 21st Century Challenges', report, New York: UNDP http://magnet.undp.org/new/pdf/gender/wpp/women_book.pdf, 2000.

United Nations Office of the Special Adviser on Gender Issues and Advancement of Women (UNOSAGI), 'Gender Mainstreaming: An overview', report, New York: United Nations, 2002.

World Bank Gender and Development Group, 'Gender Equality and the Millennium Development Goals', report, Washington: World Bank,2003.

Yuval-Davis, N., 'Women, Citizenship and Difference', *Feminist Review,* 1997, 57: 4-27.

Zuckerman, E., 'Engendering Poverty Reduction Strategy Papers (PRSP's): the issues and the challenges', *Gender and Development,* 2002, 10 (3): 88-94.

——, 'Engendering Poverty Reduction Strategy Papers (PRSP's): Why it Reduces Poverty and the Rwanda Case', paper for WIDER Development Conference on Debt Relief, Helsinki, 2001, August 17-18.

5

Human Rights

The twentieth century has been a century of democratic upsurge. Classical forms of imperialism and colonialism were over-thrown in Asia and Africa in course of struggles for liberation. Right to independence of nations and self-determination of people acquired the status of basic human rights.

The close relationship between peace and human rights as well as peace and development is clearly recognized by the charter of the United Nations which, in its preamble, declares: 'We the people of the United Nations, determined to save succeeding generations from the scourge of War [...] and to reaffirm faith in fundamental human rights...'. Article 55 adds further that, with a view to the creation of conditions of stability and well being which are necessary for peaceful relations among Nations, the United Nations shall promote conditions of economic and social progress and development and at the same time universal respect for, and observance of, human rights and fundamental freedoms.

What new elements and changes can be observed in relations between human rights, peace and development at the beginning of the twenty first century? One of the profound changes in international relations and within states is the new agenda adopted by the United Nations which finds its expression in the series of world conferences organized in the 1990s and also in new activities and programmes undertaken by the whole United Nations system.

The end of cold war and ideological confrontation, the wave of democratization and the fall of totalitarian and authoritarian regimes in many parts of the world have resulted in the addition to the already existing list of a new human rights dimension – democracy. The Vienna World Conference on Human Rights (June 1993) was convened to consider, inter alia, the relationship between development, democracy and the universal enjoyment of all human rights. The Vienna Declaration and programme of Action adopted by this Conference, in its preamble, speaks about the aspirations of all peoples for an international order founded on promoting and encouraging respect for human rights and fundamental freedoms for all, respect for the principles of equal rights and self determination of peoples, as well as for peace, democracy, justice, equality, rule of law, pluralism, development, better standards of living and solidarity. The Declaration further states that democracy, development and respect for human rights and fundamental freedoms are inter dependent and mutually reinforcing.

There is no doubt that only democracy can truly guarantee human rights. It is a political system which best allows for the free exercise of individual rights.

However there is also the other side of the linkage between democracy and human rights: "Democracy cannot be established without respect for human rights". It is a universally recognized ideal as well as a goal. It is thus a basic right of citizenship.

By the end of the twentieth century, the international community not only confirmed the close relations and interdependence existing between human rights, peace, democracy and development, but reinforced them and enriched them with new dimensions. This inter dependence became particularly evident in the 1990s as a result of the proliferation of internal conflicts. As a result an agenda for twenty-first century was adopted to give the importance of all human rights and puts human beings and human needs at the centre of all national and international actions and efforts.

Threats to Human Rights

* Poverty
* Social Exclusion
* Discrimination and Intolerance
* Terrorism
* Corruption.

A quarter of the world's population remains in severe poverty, inspite of the fact that poverty has been reduced in many parts of the world. Poverty means denial of chances to lead healthy, creative and long lives and to enjoy a decent standard of living, freedom and dignity. It also contradicts the ideal of free human beings enjoying freedom from fear and want, as established in the Universal Declaration of Human Rights and the International covenants of Human Rights. This can be achieved only if conditions are created whereby all human beings may enjoy their economic, social and cultural rights, a well as their civil and political rights.

All human beings as stipulated by Article 7 of the Universal Declaration of Human Rights "are equal before the Law and are entitled without any discrimination to equal protection of the Law". Discrimination is the very negation of the principle of equality and an affront to human dignity. The charter of the United Nations in Article 1, 55, and 75. Speaks three times about 'respect for human rights and for fundamental freedoms for all without distinction as to race, sex, language or religion". Article 2 of the International covenant on civil and political rights obliges the states parties to ensure the rights of all individuals' without distinction of any kind, such as race, colour, sex, language, religion, political or other opinion, national or social origin, property, birth or other status'. Neither the Universal Declaration of Human Rights nor the International Covenants define 'discrimination'.

Since 1946, all the United Nations organs dealing with human rights have been actively involved in the struggle against discrimination. Questions linked with the elimination of discrimination are permanently dealt with by the General Assembly, the Economic and Social Council, the Commission on Human Rights and the Sub-Commission on Prevention of Discrimination and Protection of Minorities. The Sub-Commission carries out studies whose aim is to ban discrimination. These studies are related, amongst others, to the right to education, the exercise of political rights, discrimination based on religion or beliefs, the elimination of racial discrimination and the rights of minorities and indigenous peoples.

Although the duty to combat all forms of discrimination is first of all imposed on and undertaken by states, the importance of participation of the United Nations system, regional organizations, national and international non-governmental organizations, all parts of civil society, and individual in the struggle against discrimination cannot be overlooked. The struggle for the elimination of all forms of discrimination and intolerance conducted by the United Nations system from the moment of its creation is a very important element in the efforts of the international community to ensure full implementation and observance of human rights. Discrimination, violation of rights of persons belonging to vulnerable groups (women, minorities, indigenous people, refugees, migrant workers and aliens) should also be seen as the cause of serious conflicts and danger for international and internal peace and stability. Although little progress is achieved in the development of international protection against discrimination but this does not mean that this system as a whole is already fully satisfactory. The struggle against all forms of discrimination and intolerance is still far from being won. Terrorism is not something a new phenomenon. The rise of terrorist practices in the nineteenth and twentieth centuries made evident the need for international cooperation to combat it.

The direct linkage between terrorism and violations of human rights was recognized by the World Conference on Human Rights (Vienna 1993) " The acts methods and practices of terrorism in all its forms and manifestations a well as linkage in some countries to drug trafficking are activities aimed at the destruction of human rights, fundamental freedoms and democracy, threatening territorial integrity, security of states and destabilizing legitimately constituted Governments".

There is a serious link between terrorism and human rights violations. Terrorism provides a severe test for the ideal of fundamental rights. It is a clear threat to the life and dignity of the individual.

Another threat to democracy, the rule of law and human rights is linked with corruption. With corruption, the development at social, economic and political level is endangered and have negative consequences for social justice and human rights. Corruption has always been a subject of attention of international and regional organization. "The General Assembly in its Resolution in Dec. 96 pointed to the links between corruption and other forms of Crime, in particular organized crime and stressed that, as this phenomenon, crosses national borders and affects all societies and economies, international cooperation to prevent and control, it is essential."

Thanks to the progress of science and technology in twenty first century, people have the possibility to live a better and longer life. Modern technologies are there to protect and improve health. But the progress is uneven and its impact on human rights also differs.

Globalization

Three major trends are the characteristics of the modern world. They are Globalization nationalism and regionalism. All of them have various implications for human rights but effect of Globalization is the strongest one.

It is the term used to characterise the processes of

growing inter-connection and inter-dependence in the modern world. It is generated by growing international, economic, cultural and political cooperation and links as well as the need to respond together to global problems which can be solved only on a global scale. Economically globalization is desirable as there is increasing, widening and deepening of international flow of trade, finance and information in a single, integrated global market. The worlds is shrinking as a result of increased human mobility and the increasing contacts between the world's people, with the availability of cheap and speedy travel, internet, fax and telephone etc.

V.A. Leary in Chapter II, on "Globalization and human rights" presents the mixed record of economic globalization, it may contribute to alleviation of Poverty, to mobilization of public opinion, to calling immediate attention to gross violations of human rights, sometimes it has less beneficial consequences for the rights of workers; in particular, women workers, migrant workers and indigeneous people. Globalization is a contributory factor of violations in many countries of the right of life, the right to protection of health, minority rights, freedom of association the right to safe and healthy working conditions and the right to a standard of living adequate for health and well being.

Although the economic dimension of globalization is most evident but it has other dimensions as well cultural and political. With the spread of economic processes, culture is also spreading at the international level. With the mass media, international ideas and values are being mixed and imposed on national cultures. As a result, a homogeneous worldwide culture is developing in the process known as "global village".

The culturally homogenizing effect of globalization, the gradual process of adopting common values and behavioural patterns, reinforces the universality of human rights, establishes ties and linkages between various parts of the world and helps to eliminate the discriminatory practices. However the mixed blessings of cultural globalization are linked to its negative consequences for the cultural rights of different groups such as minorities, women, immigrant workers etc. It also undermines existing cultural identities, weakens various ethical norms and social cohesion as well as the feeling of belonging and in response to this, the proliferation of various internal conflicts.

States bear the main responsibility for the implementation of human rights. Markets cannot replace governments in the determination including economic social and cultural as well as the right to development can be fully realized in which all human rights could be of economic, social and cultural policies, in providing social services and infrastructures, eradicating poverty, protecting vulnerable groups and defending the environment. Weak states cannot guarantee the rule of law which is an indispensable condition for the full implementation of human rights. However the most important challenge for the twenty first century is to construct an international order in which all human rights and freedoms, guaranteed for all.

Global warming threatens all of humanity with the very harms human rights were designed to prevent—destruction of life, health property, culture, means of subsistence, residence and movement. Indigenous peoples are particularly at risk because of their intimate relationship with the earth and its natural systems. Changes wrought to these systems by global warming can make life untenable for communities that depend on the environment for their food, water, shelter and cultural practices. For low-lying coastal areas, such as Bangladesh and the Maldives, a one-meter rise in sea level threatens to displace millions. Countries such as Grenada that were previously believed to be outside hurricane zones now experience devastating storms costing several years of gross domestic product. Glaciers in the Andes and Himalayas, the main source of drinking water for hundreds of millions of people, could disappear within 50 years. Africa, home to most of the world's least developed countries, is especially vulnerable to climate change, through such impacts as desertification, threats to agriculture and animal husbandry, and drought.

It is becoming apparent that climate change will have implications for the enjoyment of human rights. The United Nations Human Rights Council recognized this in its resolution 7/23(PDF) "Human rights and climate change" (28 March 2008), expressing concern that climate change "poses an immediate and far-reaching threat to people and communities around the word" and requesting the Office of the United Nations High Commissioner to prepare a study on the relationship between climate change and human rights.

The Fourth Assessment Report of the Intergovernmental Panel on Climate Change (IPCC) (2007) put it beyond doubt that the global climate system is warming and doing so mainly because of man-made greenhouse gas emissions. IPCC reports and other studies document how global warming will affect, and already is affecting, the basic elements of life for millions of people around the world. Effects include an increasing frequency of extreme weather events, rising sea levels, droughts, increasing water shortages, and the spread of tropical and vector born diseases.

Viewing the data through a human rights lens, it is clear that projected climate change-related effects threaten the effective enjoyment of a range of human rights, such as the right to safe and adequate water and food, the right to health and adequate housing. Equally, the human rights perspective brings into focus that climate change is set to hit the poorest countries and communities the hardest.

The international human rights standards serve as a guide for measures to tackle climate change, underscoring the fundamental moral and legal obligations to protect and promote full enjoyment of the rights enshrined in the Universal Declaration of Human Rights and in the core universal human rights treaties.

Traditionally, international law was based upon the vision of an international society composed of sovereign states that had supreme power over their respective territories and that created legal rules applicable to their relations only by their free will. The focal point of the whole international system was thus the concept of the state, the interests of which were the most important factors in its functioning.

This conception was directly inspired by civil law, whereby private interests predominated and the only condition was that they could not be in contradiction with the more or less vague concept of public order. Global change, which must not be represented as a sudden event but as an evolution that started at the end of the Second World War, deeply modifies this perspective. Its main consequence is the awareness that mankind has common interests that are superior to that of individual states and that are not necessarily - at least in the short-term - the sum of individual states' interests. Thus, the focal point of the whole international system centres more and more on mankind and not individual states. The protection of human rights, the peaceful uses of outer space and the oceans, the development of poor countries, and the conservation of the biosphere, which are considered as major tasks for the international community, cannot be understood if they are not founded on the concept of a common interest for mankind.

In the present circumstances the public law is concerned with the state of mankind, while private interests are those of the individual state. The emergence of mankind's common interests that is being achieved by global change must be reflected in international legal rules. This necessarily means a shift in the whole approach of international law from the states' central role towards that of the international community as a whole.

The Place and Role of the State in the International Community

While the realm of the competence of states has expanded during the last century, incorporating more and more tasks that formerly were left to private initiative (for example, teaching, health care, and guidance of economic life), a parallel evolution resulted in the modification of our conceptions of the place and the role of the state. For several decades, the justification of the power and even of the existence of states was to ensure to their subjects the enjoyment of fundamental rights, personal security, and the highest standard of living. Thus, a utilitarian approach has replaced the sacred character formerly recognized by states. The target of the competition between socialist and liberal countries in the 1960s was the improvement of the quality of life inside the two camps; the recent collapse of the Eastern systems that have lost the competition are to be explained by this utilitarian approach.

This approach naturally limits the genuine tendency of the states to exercise their power for its own sake. Other factors also contribute to such limitations. If throughout history facts could never be ignored by rulers, today they have a much larger impact on the conduct of national policies. Decisions are preempted by facts and situations stated and interpreted not only by members of royal councils or by politicians, but also by experts whose conclusions cannot be ignored: for example, scientists, economists, and sociologists. No government in the world can ignore expert opinions, in spite of their certain proportion of scientific uncertainty. Given the examples of the expansion of AIDS, the problem of the ozone layer, or global warming, no single government could refuse to take action or, at least, to publicly recognize the need of such action. Moreover, such statements and interpretations generally have an international character, based on the findings of scientists of different countries. Thus, sovereign states are more or less bound to their conduct by external factors over which they have no power.

'The impact of scientific findings is greatly intensified by the reactions of public opinion. Today, echoes of major events are heard all over the "planetary village" The rapidity of the awareness of the threatening modification of the global climate, in different countries and even in spheres that are usually not receptive to environmental matters, shows that states are not free to ignore such facts. Indeed, they are limited in their freedom to decide whether they will do anything or not. A concrete example will show the limits of their action in this field. Even if nobody would contest the sovereignty of a given African state over its territory and its wild fauna and flora, reactions within the world's opinion would prevent that state from making the decision of exterminating all the rhinoceros inside its boundaries.

It may be added that mechanisms guaranteeing the implementation of international obligations more and more incorporate into their procedure the information regarding international public opinion and sometimes even consultation with its representatives, concerned non-governmental organizations. However, the most important factor that limits state sovereignty is the unavoidable need to cooperate with others in a growing number of fields in order to solve essential problems. If such cooperation was needed in the first centuries of the existence of modern international law for political and military security, for trade and communications, nowadays no major branch of states' activities can escape it. The list of essential problems include the economy, health care, the protection of human rights development, environmental protection emergencies, meteorology, traffic and communications, the control of drugs and of terrorism: and the list gets longer and longer from one decade to another. The principle of cooperation, which was stressed on several occasions by the International Court of Justice, is in fact as much a necessity inspired by realities as a legal rule. Countries that tried to refuse such cooperation under certain regimes- the USSR, China, Iran - had to pay a heavy price later for their attempt to escape the international system. Global change still reinforces this trend and contributes by limiting the freedom of individual states to act'.

6

Multiculturalism and Citizenship

Introduction

Although multicultural citizenship in theory has focused on minority and group differentiated rights, multicultural citizenship put in practice has been structured in accordance of the universal rights and obligations towards citizenship. In this light present chapter takes to figure perceptible gap. A civic pluralist model of multicultural citizenship must not only recognize cultural difference in the public sphere but must also provide a new basis for political belonging as in the case of Australia and Canada where cultural difference is expressed within the limits of a common civic culture. This requires an 'open' political culture or 'deliberative democracy', in which political institutions and practices are open to analysis and reinterpretation and a sense of belonging persists based on less upon shared political values and more upon common membership of public debate within a political community in a nation state.

It has become common in recent years for scholars to claim that a 'crisis of citizenship' has emerged as a result of globalization and mass international migration.[1] In many countries, pluralistic populations have destabilized the whole idea of distinct and autonomous national cultures and, the veracity and the integrity of the nation state.

As a result, traditional concepts of 'universal citizenship' no longer seem capable of providing a sufficient basis for political belonging. It has become untenable for citizenship to demand political and cultural homogeneity, or to claim that it can transcend particularity[2]. Though 'multicultural citizenship', a form called as Ethnic and cultural diversity, which value of the different cultural forms is acknowledged and individuality respected and expressed.

As the debate concerning multicultural citizenship continues to be contested and within the literature, it is apparent that multicultural citizenship has been acknowledged primarily with minority or group-specific rights. It represents a considerable gap between the theory and practice of multicultural citizenship. For whereas theoretical discussions of multicultural citizenship relate primarily to minority rights, policies of multiculturalism in Australia and Canada the two most prominent examples of explicit multicultural citizenship regimes have taken the form of a 'civic pluralism', expressed in terms of the universal rights and obligations of citizenship.

Multiculturalism in these countries has been framed within the limits of a common civic culture, comprised of shared fundamental values.

This chapter aims to address this gap between theory and practice, by evaluating the possibility of understanding multicultural citizenship in terms of a citizenship for all.

Theories of Multicultural Citizenship

The best way of approaching multicultural citizenship is perhaps through outlining what multicultural citizenship is not. At its most fundamental level, multicultural citizenship involves a departure from traditional notions of citizenship, which abstract from the cultural, ethnic and other subnational identities of individuals, and view individuals solely as members of a given political community. Multicultural citizenship insists we recognize cultural difference among citizens and the unique identity of an individual. Citizens should be viewed not merely as abstracted individuals, but also as members of ethnic, cultural and other identity groups. As Charles Taylor[3] has argued, we form our identities and our conceptions as human agents through a 'dialogical' process with others in which we acquire 'rich human languages of expression'.

Concordantly, multicultural citizenship seeks to protect the integrity of the individual while recognizing that individuality is formed in a variety of social and cultural contexts[4]. In contrast to traditional notions of citizenship, which emphasize a dichotomy of the individual and the state, multicultural citizenship deals with a trichotomy composed of individuals, identity groups and the state.[5] A distinction should be made between 'radical' (or 'strong') and 'liberal' (or 'weak') theoretical versions of multicultural citizenship[6].

Radical formulations of multicultural citizenship advocate a fundamental shift in understandings of citizenship, portraying the universalism of liberal citizenship as merely the disguised particularism of dominant cultural or political groups.[7] Liberal constitutional norms protecting individual rights are, according to this view, 'an imperial yoke, galling the necks of the culturally diverse citizenry'[8]. Proponents of the radical version argue for a 'differentiated citizenship', which reserves special rights for 'oppressed' minority groups for example, affirmative action measures to improve the educational or occupational level of disadvantaged minorities.

While one can be sympathetic toward the notion of differentiated citizenship as a measure for increasing equity, building multicultural citizenship around the notion of oppression is highly problematic. The concept of oppression, defined to encompass exploitation, marginalization, powerlessness, cultural imperialism and violence[9], is so vague it becomes exceedingly difficult to determine with any clarity which minorities should be considered 'oppressed'[10].

Even if one is to accept oppression as the basis for a notion of multicultural citizenship, the radical multicultural citizenship model leads to a fixation and homogenization of identity, since group membership becomes effectively determinative of citizenship rights[11]. Ethnic or cultural identity can become the primary identity of citizens within the polity, which can undermine a common civic bond among citizens[12]. The radical model, oversimplifies the trichotomy of identity groups, the state and individual rights into another all too easy dichotomy of identity groups and the state.

These problems to a large extent are absent from the 'liberal' version of multicultural citizenship, which mediates more adroitly the relationship between the individual, identity group and the state. Articulated most comprehensively by Will Kymlicka,[13] this approach presents multicultural citizenship as a liberal theory of minority rights, taking as its premise individual freedom as the defining principle of liberalism. It argues individual choice can only be understood in terms of a 'societal culture' understood essentially a national culture, which 'provides its members with meaningful ways of life across the full range of human activities, including social, educational, religious, recreational, and economic life, encompassing both public and private spheres'[14]. The liberal position calls for the protection of societal cultures in order to secure the 'intelligible context of choice' for individuals (Kymlicka 1995: 150). Liberal justice requires special rights recognizing and protecting the cultures of minority groups to replace the traditional 'neutral' responses to ethnic and cultural difference, colour-blindness or benign neglect.[16]

Although this conception of multicultural citizenship goes some way to eliminate the confrontation between liberal defenders of universal individual rights and proponents of radical multicultural citizenship, the notion of societal culture severely limits the scope of its reach. The definition of societal culture as national culture allows a strong distinction to be drawn between the rights of national minorities and the rights of immigrant groups. Kymlicka has argued that while steps should be taken to ensure that national minorities should be allowed the opportunity to maintain their distinct cultures, immigrants, in choosing to settle in another country voluntarily, in fact 'waive' their entitlement to access to their original societal cultures. Immigrants' claims to equal access to a societal culture should be met by enabling immigrants to integrate into 'mainstream cultures'.[17] It is difficult, however, to justify the sharp distinction between national minority rights and the rights of immigrant groups on the basis of 'societal culture'[18]. If the right to culture derives from individual autonomy, then surely no differentiations should be allowed among the value or worth of those cultures except as expressed through the activities of individuals.[19] Kymlicka's distinction between the rights of national minorities and the rights of immigrants appears to do exactly this, in the process, fatally undermining the principled case for the recognition of immigrants' cultural concerns. The utility of Kymlicka's formulation thus seems confined to the dispensation of rights to national minorities, since it fails to deal with other multicultural (i.e. immigrant, ethnic minority) claims.

A New Theory of Multicultural Citizenship

As the foregoing discussion exhibits, there are serious deficiencies within the two dominant theoretical strains of multicultural citizenship. Perhaps more significantly, theoretical discussion of multicultural citizenship has predominantly been concerned with minority or group-differentiated rights. Here, a notable gap within multicultural citizenship arises between the levels of theory and practice. This is evident upon an examination of multicultural citizenship regimes in practice in Australia and Canada/the two most prominent examples of countries with explicit multicultural citizenship policies. As Joppke has highlighted, multicultural citizenship in Australia and Canada differ 'from that of the theorist by being a citizenship for all, not just for minorities'[20]. Multicultural rights in these contexts have not been limited to specific minorities, but have been framed in terms of the entitlements of all citizens. We find in the Australian experience, for instance, that multiculturalism at the point of its initial adoption as policy was expressed in terms of allowing 'all members of our society [to] have equal opportunity to realise their full potential and must have equal access to programs and services' and 'every person . . . to maintain his or her culture without prejudice or disadvantage'.[21] Multicultural policies in Australia have always been couched in the language of universalism and integration (see, e.g. NMAC 1999). There has always been a concern within Australia that multicultural claims be interpreted as demands for greater inclusion as citizens and not for the fragmentation of the polity into a set of strong and possibly mutually antipathetic communities.[22] Hence the emphasis on multiculturalism as enhancing social cohesion and as set within a framework of shared fundamental values. The latter has been given particular stress since the late 1980s with the emergence of a 'citizenship model' of multiculturalism.[23]

This model, articulated in the National Agenda for a Multicultural Australia report and since reaffirmed in successive Australian Government policy documents,[24] defines multiculturalism expressly in terms of the rights and obligations of citizenship. Since National Agenda, multiculturalism has been understood as conferring the right to cultural identity, but balanced by a number of limits or obligations: Multicultural policies require all Australians to accept the basis structures and principles of Australian society, the Constitution and the rule of law, tolerance and equality, parliamentary democracy, freedom of speech and religion, English as a national language and equality of the sexes.[25]

Similarly, Canadian multiculturalism has, been situated within the boundaries of common political values and structures. It would, of course, be incorrect to conflate the Canadian experience of multiculturalism with the Australian. Most notably, whereas Australian multiculturalism has essentially been a response to the ethnic and cultural diversity created by successive waves of European and Asian immigration, Canadian multiculturalism cannot be understood in isolation from the claims for recognition made by its French-speaking minority. The adoption in 1971 of a 'multiculturalism within a bilingual framework', for instance, reflects how multiculturalism has sought not only to accommodate claims made by immigrant or 'ethnic' groups, but also those made by French-speaking minorities for a form of bilingualism.[26] Perhaps more significantly, the cultural demands of the French-speaking minority in Canada have also broadened Canadian multiculturalism in ways that would not be conceivable in Australia. In contrast to Australia, where the language and vehicle of multiculturalism have been frozen, in a dialect of universal citizenship and the territory of equal and identical rights, Francophone claims for special rights have meant that multiculturalism in Canada has been understood more expansively. Nowhere is this demonstrated more clearly than by the so-called Meech Lake amendment to the Canadian constitution, which proposed the recognition of Quebec as a 'distinct society', with the possibility for variation in the interpretation of the constitution in different parts of the country.[27]

While Australian multiculturalism has been delimited by a commitment to an existing political structure and culture, Canadian multiculturalism has indeed challenged the character of the existing Canadian political system itself.

All this suggests that some sensitivity is called for when comparing Australian and Canadian multiculturalism, though it does not foreclose placing the experiences of multiculturalism in these two countries under the rubric of a multiculturalism for all.

Much like its Australian, Canadian multiculturalism stands as an integrative offer for the whole of Canadian society, anchored in the equal and identical rights of universal citizenship. This is reflected in the Canadian Multiculturalism Act, 1988, which acknowledges 'the freedom of all members of Canadian society to preserve, enhance and share their cultural heritage'. The Multiculturalism Act also states that multiculturalism is a means of promoting the 'full and equitable participation of individuals and communities of all origins' (my emphasis). That the Multiculturalism Act is subordinated to the Charter of Rights and Freedoms affirms the universalist temper of Canadian multiculturalism. Clearly the limits of multiculturalism lie within the terms of the Charter and those shared fundamental political values of Canadian citizens.

Policies in Australia and Canada reflect what might be termed a 'civic pluralist' model of multiculturalism, framed in terms of the rights and obligations of all citizens. Building on the three basic rights of citizenship expressed in T. H. Marshall's classic statement of citizenship civil, political and social, this multiculturalism adds the notion of cultural rights.[28] With respect to obligations, clear limits to diversity are imposed with the requirement that all citizens accept and commit to a shared civic culture. Thus, 'the common civic identity must transcend all particular identities while affirming people's right to maintain the particular identities they have inherited and developed insofar as these are not incompatible with that civic identity'.[29] Such expressions of multiculturalism signal a shift in the basis of national belonging from the cultural to the political, replacing specific cultural attachments with an allegiance to fundamental political principles.[30]

The emergence of this civic pluralist model of multiculturalism highlights a significant gap between the theory and the practice of multicultural citizenship. Although theoretical discussions of multicultural citizenship have focused on the need to recognize cultural difference through minority rights, policies of multicultural citizenship have sought to ensure cultural difference is expressed within a common civic culture defined as the collective assumptions about the institutions and practices within a particular political community.[31] This view on a common civic culture, however, raises an important question. Can the general type of multiculturalism practised in Australia and Canada form the basis for a new theory of multicultural citizenship; one defined not in terms of minority or group-differentiated rights but in terms of a system of universal rights and obligations?

Multicultural Citizenship and Civic Pluralism

To prusue multicultural citizenship in a form of civic pluralism has to be addressed at two levels. At the first level, civic pluralist should try citizenship needs to address demands for the acknowledgement of cultural difference within society. This is an essential requirement for multicultural citizenship, that recognises the respect owed to individuals should also extend to the culture and cultural community to which they are attached. At the second level it becomes essential for civic pluralism to encourage unity and true belonging among its citizens. Civic plularlism would be renewed according to how well it balances the need to recognize cultural difference against its impact on the legitimacy and stability of democratic cultures. Parekh has highlighted this matter as a particularly important one for a multicultural society: as otherwise it cannot act as a united community able to take and enforce collectively-binding decisions and regulate and resolve conflicts. Paradoxical as it may seem, the greater and deeper the diversity in a society, the greater the unity and cohesion it requires to hold itself and nurture its diversity.[32] It should be seen whether the civic pluralism effectively reconciles universalist principles with cultural difference. Since the implication of a cultural right of citizenship allows an individual to express his or her distinctive cultural identity, the issue here concerns whether a common civic culture, grounded in shared political values, can accommodate difference. Although the language of 'shared values' has an obvious appeal in satisfying a collective yearning for unity, it can in fact operate to belittle a multicultural society's diversity. According to Webber, if a country becomes defined exclusively by what people had in common, 'characteristics that set minority communities apart would be pushed to the margins, becoming at best protected aspects of one's personal life, at worst latent obstacles to national unity'.[33] This touches on a significant problem in grounding multicultural citizenship within a unifying civic culture. The latter, while at one level distinguishable from a broad national culture, can never be completely disentangled from its cultural context.[34] All civic and democratic cultures are embedded into specific ethnic!/national histories; even so-called 'civic' nations such as the USA and France anchor their guiding principles to a particularist legacy.[35] In the Australian context, it has been highlighted that the idea of common civic values 'involves much more than political and legal concepts, but represents a powerful affirmation of the cultural values of equity that Australians (whatever their ethnic background) are expected to share'.[36]

Hence, grounding multicultural citizenship in a shared political culture amounts to a form of 'civic assimilation' to help sustain a more or less robust national identity it acknowledges diversity without addressing the cultural asymmetries within existing political institutions.[37] Such an assessment finds some credence within Australian multicultural policies, which stress that multiculturalism does not involve a shift in Australia's political institutions or identity. The National Agenda, for instance, contained a statement that multiculturalism did not 'mean that we should dismantle or repudiate our institutions to start afresh. Our British heritage is extremely important to us. It helps to define an Australian'.[38] More recently, expressions of multiculturalism in official government statements have been subsumed under the rubric of 'Australian multiculturalism', which suggests a subordination of diversity to the notion of 'Australianness'.[39] It might be said, then, that the limits to multiculturalism effectively require of citizens an attachment to what Kymlicka called a 'societal culture', and operates to quarantine claims of difference to the private sphere.

For many prominent proponents of multicultural citizenship, this is too high a price to pay for the politics of difference.[40] It might be difficult to develop multicultural citizenship if efforts are not made to address built-in cultural biases of fundamental political institutions, which exclude citizens from diverse cultural backgrounds (Castles 1999: 36). Moreover, combining a monocultural public realm with a multicultural private realm has a tendency to work against the latter, as the public realm in every society enjoys far greater dignity and prestige.[41]

These represent significant problems with a civic pluralist model of multicultural citizenship. But they do not necessarily mean that multicultural citizenship cannot be grounded within a common civic culture. Rather, they suggest multicultural citizenship is not possible if the common civic culture is rigid and unreceptive to change. A theoretical version of a civic pluralist multicultural citizenship must deviate from the type of multicultural citizenship that exists in practice in Australia and Canada, which insists on the maintenance of an institutionally complete civic culture. A distinction here needs to be drawn between forms of civic pluralism that impose a 'closed' civic culture and forms of civic pluralism involving an 'open' civic culture. Multicultural citizenship can only sufficiently acknowledge cultural difference within an 'open' civic pluralist model, where the common civic culture is exposed to scrutiny and subject to re-interpretation.[42] As Davidson has argued, multicultural citizenship requires re-interpreting national communitarian myths and listening to the 'migrant voice', that is, incorporating the legal, political and ethical voices of multicultural citizens into the public sphere.[43] Only then can there be a common civic culture constituted by interaction between different cultural groups within the polity, in which various parties learn from and transform their respective values.[44] In effect, this challenges 'dominant' cultural groups to 'learn the ways of so-called minorities'.[45]

But can such a shared civic culture provide the basis for a new sense of belonging within multicultural societies? The idea of an open civic culture, which accepts and not merely tolerates difference, in many ways provides the basis for a more inclusive form of political identity.[46] Since the identity of the political community is defined in political rather than ethno-cultural terms, the civic pluralist model does not exclude citizens from diverse cultural backgrounds in the same way that a traditionally conceived national identity can.[47]

Moreover, the acceptance of difference within a shared open civic culture allows for members of a multicultural society to retain multiple identities as citizens.[48] Citizens can belong to different identity groups, for example, ethnic, cultural or religious, but at the same time belong to the larger polity. An open civic culture can nurture a sense of cohesion and solidarity by conferring on citizens a shared membership of a 'deliberative democracy' requiring competence in intercultural dialogues. Certainly, multicultural citizenship requires citizens to deliberate upon questions of difference, which, as a social process, is distinguishable from other kinds of communication in that it demands one to be amenable to changing one's judgments, preferences and attitudes during the course of interactions.[49] Such deliberation is underpinned by what has been labelled 'discourse ethics' by Jurgen Habermas where participants in discourse reflect on the acceptability of a proposed action for all persons who would be affected by that act. This sort of 'communicative action' presupposes a logic of 'rational communication', the aim of which is to achieve a sense of mutual understanding and recognition. Communicative acts of deliberation can be contrasted with 'strategic action', where an actor would seek 'to influence the behaviour of another by means of threats of sanctions or the prospect of gratification in order to cause the interaction to continue as the first actor desires'.[50]

Multicultural Deliberation

Multicultural deliberation might be institutionalized in a polity to formalise civic pluralism. It could firstly, generalize multicultural deliberation in public institutions of government like legislatures and the judiciary that should act as carriers of change. Legislatures, embodies institutionalized procedures for democratic polity and therefore could potentially genesis multicultural deliberation. According to Rawls, the process of law-making in strict terms should involve legislators acting in pursuit of the public interest, taking into consideration the values and norms that citizens would be reasonably expected to endorse.[51]

Parliamentary procedures of opposition, debate, questioning and investigation also incorporate a deliberative rationality, forcing the grounds on which majority parties claim to govern to be examined, challenged, tested and re-evaluated.[52]

It should be noted a number of theorists have contended that the deliberative capacity of public institutions can be located more readily within the courts rather than legislatures. For instance, in his conception of political liberalism, John Rawls has argued that the courts are the exemplars of the deliberative capacities of a polity, since they are the only branch of government that makes its decisions solely on the basis of 'public reason'.

Functioning thus, the courts act as a bulwark for the sorts of civil and political rights upon which deliberation depends, preventing them from 'being eroded by the legislation of transient majorities' or 'by organized and well-situated narrow interests skilled at getting their way' ?[53]

It is obvious that there are limits to the integration of multicultural deliberation into our public institutions. Legislatures may fail to live up to their deliberative potential. As it may be that the reality of strategic political considerations militates against the integration of deliberative habits into our parliaments. But at the same time, the courts are similarly imperfect deliberative bodies. All this is a reminder of how our public institutions cannot operate as the sole or even primary site for deliberation.[54] Certainly, multicultural deliberation needs to find roots not just merely within the law-making structures of a political community, but, more fundamentally, within the everyday practices of citizens. Multicultural citizenship is a close relative of the model of associational democracy that has been advocated with increasing voice in recent years, since it ultimately needs to be grounded within those discourses and interactions within civil society which order our understanding of the world. Multicultural deliberation demands, 'a public sphere of mutually interlocking and overlapping networks and associations of deliberation, contestation, and argumentation'.[55]

Here, a distinction needs to be made between Rawlsian or liberal conceptions of deliberative democracy and the more extensive forms proposed by the likes of Ju¨rgen Habermas and Seyla Benhabib. The Rawlsian model of deliberative democracy offers what is at best a truncated conception of deliberation. In the first instance, Rawlsian political liberalism confines deliberation to issues concerned with 'constitutional essentials' and 'questions of basic justice' namely to issues concerning the fundamental principles that pecify the general structures of government and the political process, and basic rights and liberties such as the right to vote and the freedom of association. Moreover, deliberation in so far as it is cast in terms of 'public reason' is understood not so much in terms of a process of reasoning among citizens but rather in terms of an internal dialogue with imaginary interlocutors. In addition, for Rawls, the social spaces within which public reason is exercised are strictly limited: its limits do not apply to our personal deliberations and eflections about political questions, or to the reasoning about them by members of associations such as churches and universities, all of which is a vital part of the background culture.[56]

By making such a sharp separation between a 'background culture' and a public political culture, however, the Rawlsian model pushes issues relating to the culture into the private sphere, precluding it from public consideration.[57] It upholds, in other words, the idea of a monocultural public realm. This is a fatal blow against multicultural citizenship, which requires a public diffusion of cultural dialogues and negotiations.

If there is to be a multicultural deliberative democracy, it cannot be sustained by Rawlsian public reason on the other hand it needs what Benhabib has labelled a 'dual-track' approach to deliberation incorporating multicultural dialogues into both the official public sphere and civil society.[58] The question remains whether a shared membership of a multicultural deliberative democracy, provides for the citizen a sufficient basis for belonging. It could be charged that defining political belonging in terms of a civic identity might underestimate the motivational conditions of democratic governance, in particular the need for citizens to identify with their institutions.[59] As responding to Donald Horne's call for a 'new civic faith' to replace Australian national identity, John Hirst has argued that a civic identity is a 'cold and cerebral formula' that fails to meet 'the human need for warmth and belonging'. According to Hirst, Australia should be held together by 'being Australian; by celebrating, exploring, criticizing and reassessing our Australian heritage, all the things that have defined and still define what it means to be Australian and live in this place'.[60] Other critics of multicultural citizenship in Australia similarly have suggested a civic identity tends towards a 'hollowed out notion of citizenship'[61] and dismisses the important role of an 'Anglo-Celtic core culture' in providing a sense of social cohesion and 'effective bonding cement' for citizens[62]. It is true that framing multicultural citizenship in terms of an open civic culture does not explicitly emphasize the shared history, values and customs of a particular 'people' and in this respect may fail to provide the same 'thick' sense of mutual obligation that a national identity, with its cultural power, may be able to offer.[63]

It would be wrong, however, to think that multicultural citizenship is necessarily at odds with social and political cohesion. The negotiation of difference within an open civic pluralist model of citizenship might in fact offer a novel way of achieving unity. According to Jeremy Webber, we value our polity not because we share the same values, but because we value the particular character of its public debate:

Countries always contain considerable diversity. Even the most stable and apparently unified generate vigorous debates about their very essence. In fact, societies that seem to have the clearest 'national character' are often defined more by their disagreements than by their agreements. It isn't so much what citizens agree upon as the way in which they disagree that is important. It is the distinctive structure of their fundamental debates the issues that preoccupy their public life, the ways in which those issues are posed, the kinds of solutions discussed that give a society its distinctive cast.[64]

Webber makes a very salient point in highlighting that political unity need not be expressed only through a unifying national culture or shared fundamental values. It is something that can be also understood in terms of a common commitment to public discussion through time within a political community. Civic pluralism model of multicultural citizenship cultivates exactly this kind of commitment and sense of belonging, by opening up the public sphere to inter-cultural dialogue and deliberation. This involves more than merely a superficial sense of belonging, since a citizen's commitment to public debate involves seeing the community in which the debate takes place as his or her own.[65] In time, this commitment to dialogue is likely to lead to some sharing of perspectives, of concerns, and even of answers to public questions. A multiculturally constituted civic culture 'fosters a sense of belonging among citizens and provides a shared language and body of overlapping values growing out of, and sustained by, a dialogue between them'.[66] An open civic culture, therefore, provides a sufficient basis for a new form of political belonging, by allowing for a more expansive form of political unity nurtured by diversity and deliberation.

Conclusion

This chapter has explored an ostensible gap between the theory and practice of multicultural citizenship. Whereas theoretical discussions of multicultural citizenship have predominantly focused on notions of minority rights, policies of multicultural citizenship in Australia and Canada have emphasized multiculturalism as part of the universal rights and obligations of citizenship or 'civic pluralism' multiculturalism. It has sought to answer whether this form of multiculturalism, grounded in a shared civic culture, can form the basis for a new model of multicultural citizenship. Such a model would need to not only sufficiently acknowledge cultural difference but also provide a new form of political belonging. This chapter proposes that a civic pluralist model of multiculturalism is capable of providing the foundation of a new theory of multicultural citizenship. It is possible to ground multicultural citizenship in a shared civic culture, although the latter must be exposed to critical collective reflection and re- examination. Multicultural citizenship is not possible if political institutions uphold a 'core' public culture that places pressure on diverse cultural groups to assimilate to dominant norms. It instead demands that multicultural societies be prepared to entertain shifts in their political institutions and identities. In this sense, a common civic culture might need to be understood less in terms of an allegiance to shared political values, and more in terms of the character of the public debate within a particular political community. Multicultural citizenship offers a new basis of political belonging based on citizens' shared experience in negotiating difference. Citizens within a civic pluralist model of multicultural citizenship are thus united by a shared commitment to dialogue within the polity to the 'national conversation', with all its unique and distinctive features.

What all this seems to require is a form of deliberative democracy. Multicultural citizenship calls upon citizens to deliberate upon questions of difference and such deliberation, in turn, needs to find expression in the institutions of government and the associations of civil society. Here, a balancing act that needs to be performed. Multicultural citizenship calls for a 'dual track' approach of deliberation, in which deliberation takes place in a public sphere situated within civil society, though buttressed by the norms of liberal democracy.[67] This is not without its difficulties. The notion of a 'dual track' approach to multicultural deliberation could very easily lapse into an affirmation of a liberal-democratic status quo. Yet multicultural citizenship would be impossible under such conditions, contingent as it is upon an open civic culture that is contestable through dialogue and debate. How far this contestability should extend lies at the real heart of the question of multicultural citizenship: is it enough for multicultural citizenship to insist on mere contestability within public institutions, or must it demand of them a complete rethinking and reformation? One senses the answer lies somewhere in between, but exactly what this involves raises some difficult questions.

NOTES

1. Castles and Davidson, 2000, Koopmans and Statham 1999; Joppke 1998.
2. Young, I.M., 1989.
3. Taylor, Charles, 1994, p. 32.
4. Castles, 1997, p. 13, Habermas, 3, 1994, p. 129.
5. Sachar, 1999, p. 89.
6. Faveli, 1999, Joppke, 2001.
7. Young, 1989.
8. Tully, 1995, p. 5.
9. Young, 1989.
10. Joppke, 2001; Kymlicka, 2000; Joppke and Lukes 1999.
11. Taylor, 1994, p. 71 and Rockefeller, 1994, p. 89.
12. Spinner-Haley, 1999, p. 65.
13. Kymlicka, Will, 1995.
14. *Ibid.*, p. 56.
15. *Ibid.*, p. 150.
16. Kuthakas, 1998.
17. Kymlicka, 1995, p. 113.
18. Carens, 2000 and Parekh, 1997.
19. Benhabib, 1999, p. 55.
20. Joppke, 2000, p. 446.
21. Curran, 2004, p. 32-33.
22. Kane, 2000, p. 227.
23. Castles, 1997 and Jage, 2003.
24. NMAC 1995, 1999 and DIMA 1999.
25. OMA, 1989, VIII.
26. Coulombe, 2000 and McRoberts, 1997.
27. Taylor, 1994, p. 53.

28. Marshall, T.H., 1964.
29. Kane, 2001, pp. 27-28.
30. Laborde, 2002.
31. Laborde, 2002, p. 609, and Smith 2001, pp. 4-5.
32. Parekh, 2000, p. 196.
33. Webber, J. 1994, p. 184.
34. Bader, 1997.
35. Ibid.
36. Smolicz, 1997, p.180.
37. Habermas, 1994.
38. OMA, 1989, p. 50 and NMAC 1999.
39. Curran, 2004, p. 254.
40. Taylor, 1994 and Gutmann, 1994.
41. Parekh, 2000, p. 204.
42. Kelly, 2000, p. 204.
43. Davidson, 1997a.
44. *Ibid.*, 1997b, p. 258 and Kelly, 2001, p. 233.
45. Kalantzis, 2001a, p. 120.
46. Goldberg, 1994, p. 26.
47. Arblaster 1995, pp. 195-99.
48. Hudson, 2000.
49. Dryzek, 2000, p. 11.
50. Habermas, 1990, p. 58.
51. Rawls, 1999, p. 215.
52. Behnabib, 1999, p. 72.
53. Rawls, 1999, p. 232.
54. Habermas, 1996.
55. Benhabib, 1996, p. 74.
56. Rawls, 1999, p. 215.
57. Benhabib, 2002, p. 80.
58. *Ibid.*, 2002.
59. Canovan, 2000; Laborde, 2002; Shabani, 2002.

60. Hirst, 2001, p. 117-18.
61. Galligan Roberts, 2004, p. 6.
62. Dixon, 1999, pp. 6-9.
63. See Tamir 1993 and Milles 1995.
64. Webber, 1994, pp. 185-86.
65. Webber, 1994, p. 189.
66. Parekh, 2000, p. 224.
67. Benhabib, 2002, p. 106.

REFERENCES

Anthony, Arblaster. 'Unity, Identity, Difference: Some Thoughts on National Identity and SocialUnity.' *New Community* 21 (1995): 1951, p. 206.

Bader, Veit. 'The Cultural Conditions of Transnational Citizenship: On the Interpenetration ofPolitical and Ethnic Cultures.' *Political Theory* 25.6 , 1997, pp. 771-813.

Benhabib, Seyla. 'Toward a Deliberative Model of Democratic Legitimacy.' *Democracy and Difference: Contesting the Boundaries of the Political*. Ed. S. Benhabib. Princeton, NJ, Princeton UP, 1996, 671-94.

——. "Nous" et "les Autres" The Politics of Complex Cultural Dialogue in a Global Civilization.' *Multicultural Questions* . Eds. C. Joppke and S. Lukes. Oxford: Oxford UP, 1999, 441-62.

——. *The Claims of Culture: Equality and Diversity in the Global Era*. Princeton, NJ: Princeton UP, 2002.

Canovan, Margaret. 'Patriotism is Not Enough.' *British Journal of Political Science* 30, 2000, pp. 413-32.

Carens, Joseph H. *Culture, Citizenship and Community: A Contextual Exploration of Justice as Evenhandedness*. Oxford: Oxford UP, 2000.

Castles, Stephen. 'Multicultural Citizenship: A Response to the Dilemma of Globalisation andNational Identity?' *Journal of Intercultural Studies* 18.1, 1997, pp. 51-22.

——. 'Globalisation, Multicultural Citizenship and Transnational Democracy.' *The Future of Australian Multiculturalism: Reflections on the Twentieth Anniversary of Jean Martin's The Migrant Presence*. Eds. G. Hage and R. Couch. Sydney: Research Institute for the Humanities and Social Sciences, U of Sydney, 1999. 311/41.

Castles, Stephen, and Alistair Davidson. *Citizenship and Migration: Globalisation and the Politics of Belonging*. Basingstoke: Macmillan, 2000.

Castles, S. et al. *Mistaken Identity: Multiculturalism and the Demise of Nationalism in Australia*, 2nd ed. Sydney: Pluto, 1990.

Cohen, Joshua, and Joel Rogers. 'Secondary Associations and Democratic Governance.' *Associations and Democracy*. Ed. Erik O. Wright. London and New York: Verso, 1995, pp. 71-100.

Coulombe, Pierre A. 'Citizenship and Official Bilingualism in Canada.' Citizenship in Diverse Societies . Eds. Will Kymlicka and Wayne Norman. Oxford: Oxford UP, 2000, pp. 2731-93.

Crowder, George. 'The Liberal's Dilemma.' *The Drawing Board (Digest)* 7 Mar. 2003 B/http://www.econ.usyd.edu.au/drawingboard/digest/0303/crowder.html!/.

Curran, James. *The Power of Speech: Australian Prime Ministers Defining the National Image*. Carlton, Vic: Melbourne UP, 2004.

Davidson, Alistair. 'Multiculturalism and Citizenship: Silencing the Migrant Voice.' *Journal of Intercultural Studies* 18.2, 1997a, 771-92.

——. From Subject to Citizen: Australian Citizenship in the Twentieth Century. Cambridge and Melbourne: Cambridge UP, 1997b.

Department of Immigration and Multicultural Affairs (DIMA). New Agenda for Multicultural Australia. Canberra: AGPS, 1999.

Dixson, Miriam. *The Imaginary Australian: Anglo-Celts and Identity, 1788 to the Present*. Sydney: UNSWP, 1999.

Dryzek, John S. *Deliberative Democracy and Beyond: Liberals, Critics and Contestations*. Oxford: Oxford UP, 2000.

Favell, Adrian. 'Comments on Glazer, Schain, and Fassin: How Can We be European?' *Multicultural Questions*. Eds. Christian Joppke and Steven Lukes. Oxford: Oxford UP, 1999, pp. 2421-57.

Galligan, Brian, and Winsome Roberts. *Australian Citizenship*. Carlton, Vic.: Melbourne UP, 2004.

Goldberg, David H. 'Multicultural Conditions.' *Multiculturalism: A Critical Reader*. Ed. David H. Goldberg. Boston: Blackwell, 1994.

Gutmann, Amy. 'Introduction.' *Multiculturalism: Examining the Politics of Recognition*. Ed. Amy Gutmann. Princeton, NJ: Princeton UP, 1994, pp. 31-33.

Gutmann, Amy, and Dennis Thompson. *Democracy and Disagreement*. Cambridge, MA: Harvard UP, 1996.

Habermas, Jurgen. *Moral Consciousness and Communicative Action* . Trans. Christian Lenhardt and Shierry W. Nicholsen. Cambridge, MA: MIT P, 1990.

——. 'Struggles for Recognition in the Democratic Constitutional State.' *Multiculturalism: Examining the Politics of Recognition*. Ed. Amy Gutmann. Princeton, NJ: Princeton UP, 1994, pp. 1071-48.

——. *Between Facts and Norms: Contributions to a Discourse Theory of Law and Democracy*. Trans. William Rehg. Cambridge, MA: MIT P, 1996.

Hage, Ghassan. *Against Paranoid Nationalism: Searching for Hope in a Shrinking Society*. Annandale: Pluto, 2003.

Hirst, John. 'More or Less Diverse.' *Unity and Diversity: A National Conversation (The Barton Lectures)*. Ed. Helen Irving. Sydney: ABC, 2001, pp. 1101-29.

Horne, Donald. *Public Culture: An Argument with the Future*. London: Pluto, 1994.

——. 'Something Fishy in the Mainstream?' *Unity and Diversity: A National Conversation (The Barton Lectures)*. Ed. Helen Irving. Sydney: ABC, 2001, pp. 11-19.

Hudson, Wayne. 'Differential Citizenship.' *Rethinking Australian Citizenship*. Eds. Wayne Hudson and John Kane. New York: Cambridge UP, 2000, p. 151.

Jayasuriya, Laksiri. *Immigration and Multiculturalism in Australia*. Nedlands, WA: School of Social Work and Social Administration, U of Western Australia, 1997.

Joppke, Christian. 'Immigration Challenges the Nation-State.' *Challenge to the Nation-State: Immigration in Western Europe and the United States*. Ed. Christian Joppke. Oxford: Oxford UP, 1998, pp. 51.

——. 'Multicultural Citizenship: A Critique.' *European Journal of Sociology* 42.2 , 2001, pp. 4311-47.

Joppke, Christian, and Steven Lukes. 'Introduction: Multicultural Questions.' *MulticulturalQuestions*. Eds.

Christian Joppke and Steven Lukes. Oxford: Oxford UP, 1999, pp. 11-26.

Jupp, James. 'Does Australia Need a National Identity?' Australian Identities. Ed. David Day. Melbourne: Australian Scholarly Publishing, 1998, pp. 2231-36.

Kalantzis, Mary. 'Civic Pluralism and Total Globalisation.' *Republics of Ideas: Republicanism, Culture, Visual Arts*. Eds. Brad Bucklet and John Conomos. Annandale: Pluto and Artspace Visual Arts Centre, 2001a, pp. 1101-23.

——. 'Recognising Diversity.' *Reconciliation, Multiculturalism, Identities: Difficult Dialogues, Sensible Solutions*. Eds. Mary Kalantzis and Bill Cope. Altona, Vic.: Common Ground Publishing, 2001b. 111/25.

Kane, John. 'Communitarianism and Citizenship.' *Rethinking Australian Citizenship*. Eds. Wayne Hudson and John Kane. New York: Cambridge UP, 2000. 2151/30.

Kelly, Duncan. 'Multicultural Citizenship: The Limitations of Liberal Democracy.' *Political Quarterly* 71.1, 2000, pp. 31-41.

Kelly, Paul J. '"Dangerous Liaisons": Parekh and "Oakeshottian" Multiculturalism.' *Political Quarterly* 72.4, 2001, pp. 4281-36.

Koopmans, Ruud, and Paul Statham. 'Challenging the Liberal Nation-State? Postnationalism, Multiculturalism, and the Collective Claims Making of Migrants and Ethnic Minorities in Britain and Germany.' *American Journal of Sociology* 105.3, 1999, pp. 652-96.

Kukathas, Chandran. 'Liberalism and Multiculturalism: The Politics of Indifference.' *Political Theory* 26.5, 1998,

686-99.

Kymlicka, Will. *Multicultural Citizenship: A Liberal Theory of Minority Rights*. Oxford: Oxford UP, 1995.

——. 'A North American View.' (Review symposium: report of the Commission on the Future of Multi-Ethnic Britain: UK, North American and Continental European perspectives). *Journal of Ethnic and Migration Studies* 26.4 , 2000, 723-33.

Laborde, Cecile. 'From Constitutional to Civic Patriotism.' *British Journal of Political Science* 32, 2002, 591-612.

Love, Peter. 'National Identity and Citizenship.' *Australian Identities*. Ed. David Day. Melbourne: Australian Scholarly Publishing, 1998, pp. 212-21.

Marshall, Thomas H. Class, *Citizenship and Social Development: Essays by T. H. Marshall*. New York: Anchor Books, 1964.

McRoberts, Kenneth. *Misconceiving Canada: The Struggle for National Unity*. Toronto: Oxford UP, 1997.

Miller, David. *On Nationality*. Oxford: Clarendon P, 1995.

National Multicultural Advisory Council (NMAC). *Multicultural Australia: The Next Steps, Towards and Beyond 2000*. Canberra: AGPS, 1995.

——. *Multiculturalism for a New Century: Towards Inclusiveness* . Canberra: AGPS, 1999.

Office of Multicultural Affairs (OMA). *National Agenda for a Multicultural Australia*. Canberra: AGPS, 1989.

Parekh, Bhikhu. 'Dilemmas of a Multicultural Theory of Citizenship.' *Constellations* 4.1 , 1997, pp. 54-62.

——. *Rethinking Multiculturalism*. Basingstoke: Macmillan, 2000.

Rawls, John. *The Idea of Public Reason Revisited (with The Law of Peoples)*, Cambridge, MA: Harvard UP, 1999.

Rockefeller, Steven C. 'Comment.' *Multiculturalism: Examining the Politics of Recognition*. Ed. Amy Gutmann. Princeton, NJ: Princeton UP, 1994, pp. 87-101.

Shabani, Omid A. P. 'Who's Afraid of Constitutional Patriotism? The Binding Source of Citizenship in Constitutional States.' *Social Theory and Practice* 28.3 2002, pp. 419-44.

Shachar, Ayelet. 'The Paradox of Multicultural Vulnerability: Individual Rights, Identity Groups, and the State.' *Multicultural Questions*. Eds. Christian Joppke and Steven Lukes. Oxford: Oxford UP, 1999, pp. 87-111.

Smith, Rodney. *Australian Political Culture*. Frenchs Forest: Pearson Education, 2001.

Smolicz, Jerzy J. 'Australia: From Migrant Country to Multicultural Nation.' *International Migration Review* 31.1 (1997): 171!/86.

Spinner-Halev, Jeff. 'Cultural Pluralism and Partial Citizenship.' *Multicultural Questions*. Eds. Christian Joppke and Steven Lukes. Oxford: Oxford UP, 1999. 65-86.

Stratton, Hugh. *Race Daze: Australia in Identity Crisis*. Sydney: Pluto, 1998.

Tamir, Yael. *Liberal Nationalism* . Princeton, NJ: Princeton UP, 1993.

Taylor, Charles. 'The Politics of Recognition.' *Multiculturalism: Examining the Politics of Recognition*. Ed. Amy Gutmann. Princeton, NJ: Princeton UP, 1994, pp. 25-74.

Tully, James. *Strange Multiplicity: Constitutionalism in an Age of Diversity*. Cambridge: Cambridge UP, 1995.

Uhr, John. *Deliberative Democracy: The Changing Place of Parliament* . Cambridge and Melbourne: Cambridge UP, 1998.

Webber, Jeremy. *Re-imagining Canada: Culture, Community and the Canadian Constitution*. Kingston and Montreal: MacGill-Queen's UP, 1994.

Young, Iris M. 'Polity and Group Difference: A Critique of the Ideal of Universal Citizenship.' *Ethics* 99, 1989, pp. 250-74.

7

Democratisation

Globalization's effects on democracy have received much attention recently, though there is little consensus about what precisely those effects are or how they should be addressed. Critics are almost evenly divided among those who propose cosmopolitan solutions and those who favor reinvigorating democracy at the state level. This chapter argues that we are not prepared to decide such issues because current analyses of the problem confuse globalization's effects on states with its effects on democracy and rest on problematic assumptions about the relationship between states and democracy. An alternative approach that uses globalization as a lens through which to focus on this relationship reveals that the problem is deeper and more complex than either of the existing accounts recognizes. A sound analysis of the problem must begin with a better understanding of the origins, nature, and implications of democracy's spatial and normative ties to the state and its entanglement with the modern discourse of sovereignty.

Democracy is a way of life. It's not just about

documents or governments; it's about the things we do every day that contribute to society and make it a better place to live.

The world order is rapidly changing due to global structures of production, trade and communication, it is often contended. Increasingly, the world is becoming one through the revolution in telecommunication, in transportation and in the formation of global financial markets. These three revolutions have made capital and information available everywhere and made possible world wide mass-media and culture production. Especially in the economic area this process is catching on, as world financial and banking centres fuse into one integrated network. The world financial markets constitute a fully global economy, while trade to a large degree remains regionalized. Globalization poses problems for national democracy because collective decisions are made in contexts beyond governmental control, and because it narrows down the options available for democratic elected boards. Economic globalization creates problems for established institutions and for the prevailing world system. However, a new political order may be considered to adopt.

The task is to reformulate democratic theory in order to grasp the erosion of state autonomy and to conceptualize a new political order. Thus the political dimension of globalisation is in focus and this offers interesting perspectives on both the challenges and the possibilities facing the world at the turn of the century.

Globalization implies two distinct phenomena. First, it suggests that political, economic and social activities are becoming increasingly inter-regional or intercontinental in scope. Secondly, it suggests that there has been an intensification of levels of interaction and interconnectedness between states and societies. Citizenship, as one of the foundational concepts of the modern liberal democratic states, provides the normative framework within which globalization debates may be understood and evaluated. It also examines how different concepts, theories and practices of citizenship are evolving in response to globalization. Central questions explored in this text are:

- How does globalization challenge traditional conceptions of citizenship in specific respects?
- How is globalization creating new citizenships or new civil society spaces?
- How is transnational citizenship developing and what problems are associated with it in specific areas?

The political project of extending democracy to the global level is seen as the next major challenge for proponents of democracy. Democracy as a principle has become the universal global concept for political systems. One can observe an at least formal adaptation of democratic structures around the globe. Through an increasing complexity international relations change faster and are harder to overview. In this context the impact of economic globalization is an omnipresent phenomenon in the public sphere. Globalization can be analysed with the help of different theories: Some come to the conclusion that it is a positive development for most people; others point out strong negative consequences. In turn some argue it is a completely new phenomenon, some say it is an old phenomenon existing for centuries.

Views on the positive or negative impact of

globalization are also highly polarized. Proponents credit globalization with promoting global prosperity, peace, stability, and democracy. Critics, however, attribute to globalization a long list of societal ills, including rising inequality and poverty, environmental mismanagement, and the narrowing of the scope of democracy. Some even view it as a veil for imperialist domination of the developing world. The global cultural interconnectedness that has expanded with the rise of economic interconnectedness is also often viewed as Western cultural imperialism. Some, however, reject this view. Anthony Giddens, for example, claims that global economic and cultural influences are mutual since, as the West is increasingly influenced by the rest of the world, "reverse colonialism" has become more common. Others contend that, along with economic boundaries, cultural boundaries are coming down and culture without space is emerging. Claims of cultural hybridization or cultural deterritorialization, however, grossly understate the disparity in the levels of influence reflected in the imbalance of the control of capital, technology, and media outlets between the advanced West and the developing world.

Globalisation is a highly contested term. It is a very complex process that can be understood in different perspectives: economic, political and cultural. Globalisation is a deeply differentiated phenomenon that embeds continuous processes and pattern of interaction in diverse areas of human activities – economic, social, political, cultural, military, environmental and citizenship, and through these web of activities, nation-states, societies, international institutions, NGOs, multinational corporations are linked and networking together towards achieving their objectives. Held perceives globalisation, as 'akin to a process of "structuration" in so far as it is a product of both the individual actions of, and the cumulative interactions between, countless agencies and institutions across the globe.'[1] Indeed, the impact of globalisation differs in degree and scope from one society to another. Originally, the idea of globalisation stems from the historically rapid integration of the world through the development of communication technologies and the ascendancy of international capitalism.Globalisation has three overlapping dimensions: ethical, political-economic, and cultural. The ethical dimension is concerned with the question of citizenship in the international laws. The politico-economic deals with trans-nationalisation of capitalist market forces in which there is a global interconnectedness in trade and commerce. These dimensions mean that globalisation as with democracy has never been given any fixed and globally acknowledged conceptualisation.

Globalisation simply means—many things to many people. Moreover, since the beginning of the much stated waves of democracy across the world—from southern Europe to Eastern Europe, from south Asia to Latin America and down to Africa, students of democratisation began to establish the links between globalisation and democratisation. It is important to note that *democratisation in itself is globalisation*. It is globalisation because it accentuated the transformation of a global political economy in which hitherto closed economies dictated by authoritarian regimes were brought into a mutual interdependence through economic and political interconnectedness. In similar perspective, McGrew refers to globalisation as the 'multiplicity of linkages and interconnections between the states and societies which make up the modern world system. It describes the process by which events, decisions and activities in one part of the world can come to have significant consequences for individuals and communities in quite distant parts of the globe.'[2]

Infact Held observes that globalisation entails two phenomenal issues: first it entails networks of political, economic and social activities that are becoming interregional and intercontinental in scope. Second it entails a more intensification of degree of interaction between states and societies.[3] The intensification and interconnectedness of states and societies especially from late 1990s have been conditioned by the rapid development of communication technologies and the sophistication of the international capitalism. The globalisation of capitalist forces through the activities of multinational corporations, the IMF, World Bank, World Trade Organisation, UN, other international organisations (bilateral and multilateral) and even relations between developed economies and underdeveloped ones have invariably made it relatively easier for the spread of democracy. Democracy is the system of governance through which smooth, effective, efficient and harmonious global interaction is possible. In this context Held defines globalisation "as a spatial phenomenon, lying on a continuum with 'the local' at one end and "the global" at the other.[4] It denotes a shift in the spatial form of human organisation and activity to transcontinental or interregional patterns of activity, interaction and the exercise of power. It involves a stretching and deepening of social relations and institutions across space and time such that, on the one hand, day-to-day activities are increasingly influenced by events happening on the other side of the globe and, on the other, the practices and decisions of local groups or communities can have significant global reverberations.

There is a striking paradox to note regarding the contemporary era: from Africa to Eastern Europe, Asia to Latin America, more and more nations and groups are championing the idea of democracy; but they are doing so at just that moment when the very efficacy of democracy as a national form of political organisation appears open to question. Indeed, one would concur that globalisation is rendering the efficacy of state sovereignty rather irrelevant but absolutely one must be cautious in over-stretching the idea of loosening efficacy of democracy. This is perhaps because of the fact that global interactions in economic and political spheres have predated the modern system and pattern of globalisation. And as long as states continue to participate in such interactions, they certainly would continue to lose substantial degree of their autonomy. The traditional rule of international politics is that international conventions, treaties and resolutions bind states. Although one may argue that economic and military powers are important determinants of states interaction. But irrespective of these power potentials, the degree of sovereignty would continue to be questioned through the traditional interactions.

Moreover, contemporary waves of democratisation are one of the several consequences of globalisation. Explaining globalisation and democratisation as a cause-effect relationship makes the argument of economic pre-condition thesis of democracy very important. Today there seems to be a common understanding that there is an extensive trade, finance and production relations amongst societies. These global politico-economic networks have made economic and political liberalisation relatively easier. Thus the global politico-economic liberalisation has according to Grugel[5] links with democratisation in some pertinent ways: first, it establishes the ascendancy and authority of western capitalism over the developing world, thereby reducing their politico-economic options. Through repeated interactions developing societies and former communist societies are continuously subjected to political aid conditionality. These societies are webbed into a particular development strategy in which only 'liberal democracy' and economic openness are the way forward. No wonder therefore that the world witnessed the growth of democracy in such an unpredictable number. Democratisation has consequently become a process of continual hegemony of developed countries over the developing ones. Secondly, globalisation encourages democratisation because economic liberalisation in form of trade creates a free global market that facilitates new form of citizenship, middle class and civil society, which classical democracy theorists contend to be engines of democratisation. Liberalisation led to political changes and reforms in several states and it also usually affects the capacity and capability of autocratic regime through formal and informal reduction of its financial base and empowering the dissenting groups. Liberalisation in this way leads to democratisation.

Conversely, the politico-economic global networks have influenced in disgust the rapid development of democracy in several countries, especially in sub-Saharan Africa. The effects of liberalisation have continuously weakened the political spirit of states, weakened the economic potentialities of people, as well as exclude the poor from political and economic participation, making them impotent in the democratisation process. Globalisation has contributed to the global polarisation of states. It widens the North-South divide. Developed states have continued to be rich and the developing countries have continued to be poor as well.

The global wave of democratisation, which has been affected by international forces, according to Schwartzman[6] heralded a paradigm shift in the contemporary scholarship of democracy. The wave was quite staggering in that it includes countries with more than half a century of non-democratic rule and some that had substantial democratic interludes; it includes countries that suddenly obstruct their traditional authoritarian regimes, populist dictatorship and bureaucratic ones, and also comprises those that took radical measures, like assassination, dismantling of symbols of authoritarianism, and radical uprising against military and in some instances military relinquishing power honourably. In view of this staggeringly wide spread of democracy Schwartzman among others, linked the democratisation phenomenon with contemporary globalisation. Accordingly, he examined several ways in which globalisation impacted on democracy. He maintained that the volume of analysis of global linkages have presented a *prima facie* evidence that connotes that contemporary democratisations are not isolated, coincidental nor randomly distributed in time and space. Thus, the global factors of democratisation could be classified into six—

1. *Favourable international climate:* this means that democratisation in one country leads to democratisation in another. Huntington[7] calls this snowballing effect, where a favourable global

atmosphere led to a diffusion of democratic ideas, through the expansion of global communication and transportation (e.g. satellites, computers, faxes, etc.). The spread of democracy in eastern and southern Europe following the collapse of socialist command political economy is good example. Unfortunately this factor neglects the role of other equally important factors, such as economic, social and political factors, which are global and local in perspectives.

2. *Global industrialisation and development:* this perspective stresses the significance of global economic development as promoting global democratisation. The triumph of international capitalism has eliminated the growth of pre-capitalist niches and led to capital-intensive technological production. Schwartzman[8] calls this a 'convergence', because the pre-existing differences between industrialised and non-industrialised societies are disappearing. Put differently, global industrialisation led to the growth of professional, middle and working classes, which are agents of democratisation. Although, all these global factors carry weight in the analysis of globalisation and democratisation, it is vital to note that these plethoras of factors actually have widened the gap between the rich and the poor in developing countries. The current degree of poverty is an empirical illustration that undermines the positivists' claim of globalisation bringing in convergence for democratisation. In most of these societies, the percentage of poor people has continued to rise; social services are degenerating

by the day and consequently democratic credentials are losing moral support. Also one can argue that the perceived gains of international capitalism are yet to bring democracy to Middle East, which further questioned the viability of the argument of global capital. Although, it could still be argued that the Middle Eastern countries are heavily dependent on economic resource (oil) and not particularly well integrated into the global economy.

3. *Global shock:* Schwartzman[9] argues that global shocks have contributed to democratisation by creating legitimacy crises in authoritarian regimes. Global shocks include the 1929 world depression, which triggered the fall of oligarchic regimes in Latin America and the 1973 and 1979 oil crises. The former heralded democratisation in the Philippines, Spain, Portugal, Greece, Brazil and Uruguay, while the latter according to Huntington[10] fuelled the *Third Wave* and in some countries such as United States, France, Canada, West Germany, ruling parties lost elections.Similarly, Frieden[11] argues that the 1980s debt crisis was one of these shocks that caused legitimacy crises and the subsequent collapse of autocratic regimes in several developing countries, especially in the Latin America. Against this background, if global shocks in economic recession (oil price crisis and depression), could fuel re-democratisation in other countries, certainly one should equally anticipate that oil price windfall during the 1970s should boost democratisation process in oil producing states.

4. *Foreign intervention:* direct and indirect foreign interventions have contributed for democratisation in several countries. Currently, the political conditionality attached to the provision of aid is an example of direct foreign intervention. The U.S. Japan and other European democracies are quite prominent in the provision of 'conditional aid'. Schwartzman[12] stresses that 'in 1991 and 1992, the US and the Paris club declared a moratorium on aid to Kenya and Malawi pending the implementation of political reforms such as multiparty democracy, cessation of politically motivated torture and imprisonment and the like.' Similarly, Roquie[13] observes that 'the hemispheric policy of successive US administrations—the alternation after 1914 between anti-communist vigilance and democratising preoccupations—imparts a rhythm to the phases of autocracy and the waves of demilitarisation.' Today, many international organisations such as the World Bank, IMF, London club and Paris club, etc. have joined the bandwagon of conditional aid provision to institutionalise political reforms in developing countries. However, more often than not countries that receive aid do not adhere strictly to the conditions and there is no way to determine the extent to which recipient nations are actually implementing the aid conditions.

5. *Shifting global hegemony:* this factor is nevertheless related to the above. It emphasises the global impact on democratisation in terms of a shift of economic and political hegemony from one international power to another. The process of

the shifts is expected to trigger democratisation in some countries. Perhaps due to global interconnection that bound countries together. For instance, Wallerstein[14] argues that the collapse of communist bloc was never a result of triumph of western democracy, but a consequence of the decline of United States' hegemony, thereby allowing the USSR to maintain monopoly over communist bloc. On the other hand, the US economy was challenged by economic developments in Japan and Germany, which resulted in the collapse of its economic and political hegemony. This ultimately led to the spread of democracy to other angles of the world. One would agree that the world has witnessed the emergence of more capitalist societies with the growth of Japan and German economies though there has not been any power shift in the world economic order. United States is still a power to be reckoned with in international political and economic matters. Perhaps, Japan and recently the formation of regional blocs such as European Union could be a check on the perceived US excesses in international issues. One can thus contend that the universal trend toward regional organisations help in contemporary democratisation. For example, any member of such organisation would face penalties for undemocratic attitudes, as democratisation is a pre-condition for membership.

Viewing the shifting global hegemony differently, Schwartzman[15] contends that it gave rise to new capitalist class and led to urban migration and proliterianisation of a section of the peasantry.

As a result, it increases the level of class conflict. These transformations bred new pro-democracy coalition, which mark the beginning of democratisation in many societies, such as Portugal.

6. *World-system cycles:* this model argues on the systemic and cyclical nature of the international system that has affected global democratisation. The world-system according to Arrighi[16], develops through cycles: accumulation (capital accumulation and consolidation) – disintegration. This factor is concerned with the intensification of inter-capitalist competition, which is associated with reorganisation of production and perhaps a shift in hegemonic dominance. For instance, there was a hegemonic shift from Britain to US in 19 th century. The *Third Wave* democratisation has been affected by these changes. Similarly Bergesen[17] argues that economic stagnation and its associated socio-political repercussions forced developing countries to reconstitute their internal political and economic policies in the hope of overcoming the problems of slow growth, inflation, poverty, unemployment and international debt. Through this restructuring, democratisation spread to developing countries.

Finally, based on these six global factors, which have formidably explained the relationships between globalisation and democratisation, Schwartzman[18] notes 'class conflict as the social mechanism linking world-system processes to national political dynamics. In this framework, domestic political structures become part of the evolving transnational fabric of economic relations', which have profound impact on democratisation in developing countries. The factorisation of international impact on democratisation by Schwartzman offers a deterministic approach to understanding globalisation and democratisation. However, the relationship between these two global phenomena is beyond this simple deterministic and yet lineal approach. The factors have not told us the impact, if any, of democratisation on globalisation. Premised on this, Plattner[19] perceives globalisation and democratisation as mutually reinforcing agents with a symbiotic relationship. He therefore notes that 'although both globalisation and democratisation have long and complex histories, each was greatly accelerated by the collapse of soviet communism in the revolutions of 1989-91. These two trends have been interrelated and, for the most part, mutually reinforcing. That is to say, globalisation has fostered democratisation and democratisation has fostered globalisation.' To clarify the ambiguity, Plattner[20] emphasises that the domination of the world by the international capitalist ideology is more favourable to globalisation than the reverse.

Liberal democracy on the other hand favours the economic arrangements in the form of contemporary free market organisations that engender globalisation. Interestingly, democracy's central attributes of freedom, liberty and rights to information help in promoting the 'free' flow of information and communications that further empowered the development of globalisation. Similarly, globalisation contributes in undermining the legitimacy of authoritarian regimes by exposing their citizens to interactions with other peoples' ways of lives in the world through information and communication. In this way, it is favourable to democratisation. Despite this interwoven relationship, democracy and globalisation could be at odds with each other. As globalisation tends to eradicate national barriers between societies and dislodge effective decision-making from national level, it simultaneously threatens both authoritarian and democratic regimes. In this sense globalisation becomes inimical and hostile to democratic self-government. For example, the mass demonstration against WTO, the IMF, UN and the World Bank is a sign of this hostility. In this vein Barber (21) argues that globalisation is simply a threat to democracy as the success of globalisation in markets, labour, currency and information systems does not extend to civic and democratic institutions. Held's opinion that in international perspective globalisation has provided a golden opportunity for the creation of cosmopolitan democracy and certainly this led to the spread of democracy to many totalitarian and autocratic regimes. He argues that:

> The theory of cosmopolitan democracy is one of the few political theories, which examines systematically the democratic implications of the fact that nation-states are enmeshed today in complex interconnected relations. Our world is a world of overlapping communities of fate, where the fate of one country and that of another are more entwined than the borders of countries and challenge the relevance of those borders in key respects.[22]

Theoretically, the literature on the relationship between globalisation and democratisation could be categorised into competing positions: (a) globalisation promotes democracy (b) globalisation hampers the spread of democracy, and (c) globalisation has no impact on democracy.

The theoretical assumption that globalisation promotes democracy is based on the fact that the former engenders economic development promotes democracy. Free market economy, which is the backbone of globalisation, usually leads to economic growth and development increases the size of the middle class, promotes education, and consequently reduces income inequality, thereby leading to democratisation. Globalisation also makes necessary demand for international business activities, which need peaceful trading environment. This might have been part of the reasons why foreign investors are keen about security in Third World for their continued investment. This perspective, The International Financial Institutions (IFIs), donor agencies and states always impose political and economic conditionalities for aid to the developing world. Through this process, democracy would ultimately spread to these states because of internal need for aid and international demand for adjustment and political reforms. The effect of this led to another factor: that because of this, the autocratic regimes in developing countries easily loose support and their power steadily erode. They no longer enjoy support from the international system in which their respective countries are unavoidably members. Thus, democratisation simply becomes irresistible. This factor affects the nature of contact of countries in the global system. For example, in view of the magnitude of globalisation, autocratic regimes would no longer have formidable power over the activities of international private and public organisations, as well as the international media. With increasing global networks, the global information agencies such the radio, television, Internet, newspapers and satellites are making information easily accessible to ordinary citizen thereby inducing democratic ideas that make democratisation reforms absolutely necessary in these countries. This is a fortunate situation, which the autocratic regimes cannot control. In similar perspective, globalisation indeed, strengthens the activities of the domestic NGOs and civil society advocating for democratisation, and it leads to appropriate diffusion of democratic ideas and aspirations especially following the *Third Wave* of democratisation.

The theoretical assumption that globalisation hampers democracy notes that it obstructs the autonomy and sovereignty of states especially in terms of public policies that would positively affect its citizens and strengthen the democratisation processes. This is done by the state's concern in satisfying foreign investors. The activities of MNCs and other IFIs in developing world further threaten the economic growth and development of these societies, because capital is daily repatriated to the developed world. This has the effect of disjointing the internal developmental activities of these states and thus negatively affects their democratisation process. Specifically, globalisation weakened the economic power of the local bourgeoisies. These reasons could lead to serious economic crises that might hinder the development of democracy. In the current situation Third World societies are facing poverty-related problem, which certainly is threatening the sustainability of their democratisation process. Quan and Reuveny contend that globalisation induces labour migration across societies, irrespective of how the residents typically would attempt to restrict or eliminate immigrants in the political system to reduce political competitiveness.[23] This factor reminds one of how at the eve of general elections, May 5, 2005, the issue of immigration has become a strong factor in the British Parties' campaign processes. For example, the Conservative Party has included the issue in their campaign manifesto. Nick de Bois (Conservative candidate for Enfield North) contends that 'asylum and immigration – Enough is enough. Britain is stretched to breaking point and our local hospitals, schools and housing are suffering'[24]. Norris has after a presenting a graphical data showing how the race and immigration question grew rapidly over the years form 1974-2005 from 10-28% respectively to become a political issue, captured the scenario well, when he writes that the 'conservatives' [party] strategy is similar to that used by many other European centre-right parties when confronted by a popular threat from their xenophobic rivals.'[25] This is the effect of globalisation. This in a way affects the British democracy *per se*. But importantly it tells much on its image as an advocator and champion of democracy the world over. Globalisation continues to widen the gap between the North and the South and this invariably obstructs the democratisation process in the South who might view the democratisation agenda as not only solving their basic problems but also as a way of further subjecting them to satisfy the need of the international division of labour.

In sum, the assumption that globalisation doesn't affect democracy, depicts that globalisation is a *buzzword*, whose effect has been over exaggerated. The world economy is never integrated, MNCs have their home base and FDI (Foreign Direct Investment) concentrates only in few countries, and thus globalisation won't affect their democracy[26]. Contemporarily, to say that globalisation doesn't affect any country's democracy, weather developed or developing, is simply a mere naivety, unnecessary narrow mindedness and theoretical misunderstanding of the idea of globalisation. Interestingly, Quan and Reuveny[27], in an empirical study on the interface between economic globalisation and democracy of 127 countries from 1970-1996, summarily discovered that:

> trade openness and portfolio investment inflows exert negative affect on democracy. The negative effect of trade is constant over time whereas the effect of portfolio investments strengthens. FDI inflows affect democracy positively, but the effect weakens over time. The spread of democratic ideas promotes democracy persistently over time. Theses patterns hold for all countries. In sum, the economic aspects of integration into the world economy are beginning to cause a decline in national democratic governance.

From the above brief survey of the linkages between globalisation and democratisation, treating the former as an independent variable, one can adduce divergent views on the role of globalisation on democratisation. Thus, treating the issue in this way only curtails our supposed comprehensive understanding of globalisation and democratisation. It is on this premise, theoretically understand the twin issues, we must dialectically treat the effect of globalisation on democratisation. Dialectical investigation is important in that it enables one to measure the extent to which states embrace the fruits of global-democratisation and strategies put in place to contain the hurdles of globalisation.

NOTES

1. Held, D., McGrew, A., Goldblatt, D., and Perraton, J. (1999) *Global Transformations: Politics, Economics and Culture* (Cambridge: Polity Press). p. 27.
2. McGrew, A.G., Lewis, P.G. et al (1992) *Global Politics: Globalisation and the Nation-states* (Cambridge: Polity Press).p. 23.
3. Held, D. (2000) *Democracy and Globalisation*, p. 2.
4. *Ibid.*
5. Grugel, J. (2002) *Democratisation: A Critical Introduction* (New York: Palgrave Publishers Ltd.). pp. 117-119.
6. Schwartzman, K.C. (1998) 'Globalisation and Democracy', *Annual Review of Sociology*, Vol.24, pp. 160-161.
7. Huntington, S.P. (1991) *The Third Wave: Democratisation in the Late Twentieth Century* (Norman: University of Oklahoma Press). p33-36
8. Schwartzman, K.C. *op.cit.*
9. Schwartzman, K.C. *op.cit.*
10. Huntington, S.P. *op.cit.*, p. 51.
11. Frieden, J. (1991) *Debt, Development and Democracy* (Princeton, NJ: Princeton University Press).p63
12. Schwartzman, K.C., *op.cit*, p. 170.
13. Roquie, A. (1996) 'Demilitarisation and the Institutionalisation of Military-dominated Politics in Latin America' in O'Donnell, Scmitter, P.C. and Whitehead, L. (Eds.) *Transitions from Authoritarian Rule: Comparative Perspective* (Baltiomore, MD: Johns Hopkins Press), p. 126.
14. Wallerstein, I. (1991) *Geopolitics and Geoculture* (Cambridge: Cambridge university Press).
15. Schwartzman, K.C. *op.cit*, p. 173-174.
16. Arrighi in Schwartzman, K.C. *op.cit.*,
17. Bergesen, A. (1992) 'Communism's Collapse: A World System Explanation', *Journal of Political Military Sociology*, Vol. 20 (summer). pp. 133-151.
18. Schwartzman, K.C. *op.cit*, p. 177.

19. Plattner, M.C. (2002) 'Globalisation and Self-Government', *Journal of Democracy*, Vol.13, No.3, p. 154.
20. *Ibid.*, pp. 58-61.
21. Barber, B. (2001) 'Can Democracy Survive Globalisation?' *Government and Opposition*, 275.
22. Held, D. (1998) 'Democracy and Globalisation' in Archibugi, D., Held, D. and Kholer, M. (Eds.) *Re-imagining Political Community: Studies in Cosmopolitan Democracy* (Cambridge: Polity Press). p. 26.
23. Quan, L. and Rueveny, R. (2000) 'Economic Globalisation and Democracy: An Empirical Analysis', Paper Presented at the International Studies Association Annual Meeting, Los Angeles, CA, and the Midwest Political Science Association Annual Meeting, Chicago. p. 13.
24. Davoudi, S. (2005) 'Tories make much of a Shrinking Issue', *Financial Times*, Thursday, 14 April. p. 4.
25. Norris, P. (2005) 'Immigration is one of the few key Policies Left for the Right', *Financial Times*, Thursday, April 14. p. 4.
26. Quan, *op.cit.*, p. 15.
27. *Ibid.*, p. 38.

Conclusion

At the beginning of the twenty-first century, the world experiences processes of both integration and disintegration. The expansion of world markets as a form of economic globalisation can be understood as a process of integration composed of international flows of capital, goods, information, and people. The same process is both a form of economical integration and a polarization of wealth that exacerbates existing tendencies toward greater global inequalities between rich and poor countries and regions. It also accentuates the need for reviewing the templates of the global system of governance that emerged with the Bretton Woods agreement, which founded many of the world institutions that comprised the architecture of the postwar world system. Now, more than at any time in the past, with the end of the Cold War, the collapse of the Soviet system, the consolidation of the EU, the entry of China in the WTO, and the growth of India, we are witnessing an accelerated set of changes—economic, cultural, technological and political—that impinge on one another in novel ways and create new possibilities and dangers both for the democratic state and the notions of citizenship and national identity that underpin it.

The modern concept of citizenship—a recent concept historically – implies the existence of a civil or political community, a set of rights and obligations ascribed to citizens by virtue of their membership in that community, and an ethic of participation and solidarity needed to sustain it. Most traditional accounts of citizenship begin with the assertion of basic civil, political and social rights of individuals and note the way in which the modern concept as inherently egalitarian, took on a universal appeal with the development of the liberal tradition which is often understood as synonymous with modernity. Yet the concept has appealed to both conservatives and radical democrats: the former emphasise individual freedom at the expense of equality and see state intervention as an intolerable and unwarranted violated of the freedom of the individual while the latter stress the democratic potential of citizenship. Increasingly, on the left the concept has been seen as a means to control the injustices of capitalism. For the left, the most pressing question has been the status of citizenship in the modern state and what kind of political community best promotes it.

The classic theorisation of democratic citizenship is to be found in Marshall's famous modelling of three forms of citizenship: civil, political and social. In this conception civil citizenship referred to personal liberty and a regime of individual rights, political citizenship referred to both political participation and democratic representation, and social citizenship to intervention by the state to reduce economic inequalities and promote social justice. It is now possible to chart the significant shifts in the definitions of citizenship that have accompanied globalization, including the breakdown of the historic compromise between capitalism, democracy and the welfare state, the rise of neoliberalism, and with it the expansion of world markets.

In the U.S. under the neocons, and the U.K. under the so-called Third Way, a mantle inherited by Prime Minister Brown, there has been a shift from the concept of rights to responsibilities and a move away from state intervention towards the market and the construction of 'consumer-citizens' who are increasingly forced to invest in themselves at critical points in their life-cycle (education, work, retirement) or go into debt. At the same time there has been a shift to the third sector with community and church involvement in the definition of social welfare policy and an emphasis on giving, gifting and voluntary work often thinly disguising a moral re-regulation of social life, especially of single women and their children. Increasingly, with the development of information and communications technologies, there has been a rise in state surveillance and, especially after 9/11, an erosion of liberal rights and a shift from active political citizenship to passive political literacy; concomitantly, the same technologies have supported new public spaces and civil networks that are interest-based and transcend the geography of face-to-face communities and even larger collectivities like states.

Perhaps, more than ever before the question of globalization and citizenship revolves around the free movement of peoples. By this mean not only the modern diaspora, or the planned colonial migrations, or the more recent global mobility of highly skilled labour that is rewarded by citizenship. But more importantly, it means refugees of all kinds and asylum-seekers and all that entails—enforced border crossings, ethnic cleansing policies, the huge illegal movement of so-called 'aliens' or the 'undocumented', detention camps the likes of Woomera in Australia and even Guantanomo Bay, where the concept of rights is fragile or has entirely disappeared.

If we wish to promote a more pluralistic, ethical citizenship, we will need to understand how societal systems, structures and practices contribute to hegemonic practices or how they may enable new possibilities for agency's self determination. The concept of being a woman interfaced with race, disability or class has the potential to displace her potential public role in society because her perceived gender status is made more visible than her personal qualities. Even today, women's relationship to men is often still defined by their gender and family position. So there is still work to be done. For instance, policy and educational practices can explore how women are socially constructed formally and informally. An ethical citizenship education would examine how much women's visibility enables a shared power relationship with men. Education for active citizenship, then depends in part on how people are taught to be regarded in society.

Citizenship is not just about a position inside or outside society. It also implies action--participation in the life, development and decisions of the community. The shifts in meanings and practice of citizenship along the lines outlined above imply an improved and more dynamic interaction between people, citizens' organisations and governance institutions. Activism promoting the interests of marginalised groups such as women has for many years challenged unequal and oppressive power relations that limit rights to full citizenship. Moblising in civil society demonstrates the involvement of groups in decisions that affect their lives and the lives of others in their communities.

Wheras theoretical discussions of multicultural citizenship have predominantly focused on notions of minority rights, policies of multicultural citizenship in Australia and Canada have emphasized multiculturalism as part of the universal rights and obligations of citizenship or 'civic pluralist' multiculturalism. It has sought to answer whether this form of multiculturalism, grounded in a shared civic culture, can form the basis for a new model of multicultural citizenship. Such a model would need to not only sufficiently acknowledge cultural difference but also provide a new form of political belonging.

Multicultural citizenship offers a new basis of political belonging based on citizens' shared experience in negotiating difference. Citizens within a civic pluralist model of multicultural citizenship are thus united by a shared comitment to dialogue within the polity to the 'national conversation', with all its unique and distinctive features.

What all this seems to require is a form of deliberative democracy.

Multicultural citizenship calls upon citizens to deliberate upon questions of difference and such deliberation, in turn, needs to find expression in the institutions of government and the associations of civil society. A balancing act needs to be performed for greater deliberation.

The terms 'globalization' and 'citizenship'are not normally juxtaposed in social and political analysis. They tend to appear as contradictory or, at least, conflicting: the former points to a set of economic and cultural processes of unequal and uneven world integration, based on the unregulated flows of capital and underwritten by developments in new information and communications technologies, while the latter serves mainly as a metaphor for political community or solidarity. To what extent does globalization (as financialization) threaten the sovereignty of the nation-state and with it the notion of citizenship that developed during the modern era? To what extent can citizenship be severed from questions of national identity? Within the context of globalization how can we maintain or develop a sense of community and local identity to establish or defend the hard-won entitlements of social citizenship? What possibilities are there for developing genuine transnational alliances and defining entirely new sets of rights within supranational political arenas? To what extent can the movement of individuals and peoples come to be regarded as genuinely free within states, regions, and continents; and how might states that encourage the free-floating 'globally integrated enterprise' also extend universal and lawful protections to migrants, refugees and those seeking asylum? These are critical questions that ought to inform a democratic response to citizenship and to the question of citizenship education.

Bibliography

Anthony, Arblaster. 'Unity, Identity, Difference: Some Thoughts on National Identity and Social Unity.' *New Community* 21 (1995): 195-206.

Bader, Veit. 'The Cultural Conditions of Transnational Citizenship: On the Interpenetration of Political and Ethnic Cultures.' *Political Theory* 25.6 (1997): 771-813.

Barbelet, J.M. *Citizenship: Rights, Struggle and Class Inequality*, Open University Press, 1988.

Benhabib, Seyla. 'Toward a Deliberative Model of Democratic Legitimacy.' *Democracy and Difference: Contesting the Boundaries of the Political*. Ed. S. Benhabib. Princeton, NJ: Princeton UP, 1996. 67-94.

——,'"Nous" et "les Autres" The Politics of Complex Cultural Dialogue in a Global Civilization.' *Multicultural Questions*. Eds. C. Joppke and S. Lukes. Oxford: Oxford UP, 1999. 44-62.

——. *The Claims of Culture: Equality and Diversity in the Global Era*. Princeton, NJ: Princeton UP, 2002.

Canovan, Margaret. 'Patriotism is Not Enough.' *British Journal of Political Science* 30 (2000): 413-32.

Carens, Joseph H. *Culture, Citizenship and Community: A Contextual Exploration of Justice as Evenhandedness*. Oxford: Oxford UP, 2000.

Castles, Stephen. 'Multicultural Citizenship: A Response to the Dilemma of Globalisation and National Identity?' *Journal of Intercultural Studies* 18.1 (1997): 5-22.

——, 'Globalisation, Multicultural Citizenship and Transnational Democracy.' *The Future of Australian Multiculturalism: Reflections on the Twentieth Anniversary of Jean Martin's The Migrant Presence*. Eds. G. Hage and R. Couch. Sydney: Research Institute for the Humanities and Social Sciences, U of Sydney, 1999. 31-41.

Castles, Stephen, and Alistair Davidson. Citizenship and Migration: Globalisation and the Politics of Belonging. Basingstoke: Macmillan, 2000.

Castles, S. et al. *Mistaken Identity: Multiculturalism and the Demise of Nationalism in Australia*, 2nd ed. Sydney: Pluto, 1990.

Cohen, Joshua, and Joel Rogers. 'Secondary Associations and Democratic Governance.' Associations and Democracy. Ed. Erik O. Wright. London and New York: Verso, 1995. 71-100.

Coulombe, Pierre A. 'Citizenship and Official Bilingualism in Canada.' *Citizenship in Diverse Societies*. Eds. Will Kymlicka and Wayne Norman. Oxford: Oxford UP, 2000. 273-93.

Crowder, George. 'The Liberal's Dilemma.' *The Drawing Board (Digest)* 7 Mar. 2003 B/http://www.econ.usyd.edu.au/drawingboard/digest/0303/crowder.html!/.

Curran, James. *The Power of Speech: Australian Prime Ministers Defining the National Image.* Carlton, Vic: Melbourne UP, 2004.

Dahrendorf, R. (1959) *Class and Class Conflict in Industrial Society*, London.

Davidson, Alistair. 'Multiculturalism and Citizenship: Silencing the Migrant Voice.' *Journal of Intercultural Studies* 18.2 (1997a): 77-92.

——, *From Subject to Citizen: Australian Citizenship in the Twentieth Century*. Cambridge and Melbourne: Cambridge UP, 1997b.

——, Department of Immigration and Multicultural Affairs (DIMA). New Agenda for Multicultural Australia . Canberra: AGPS, 1999.

Dixson, Miriam. *The Imaginary Australian: Anglo-Celts and Identity, 1788 to the Present*. Sydney: UNSWP, 1999.

Dryzek, John S. *Deliberative Democracy and Beyond: Liberals, Critics and Contestations*. Oxford: Oxford UP, 2000.

Favell, Adrian. 'Comments on Glazer, Schain, and Fassin: How Can We be European?' *Multicultural Questions*. Eds. Christian Joppke and Steven Lukes. Oxford: Oxford UP, 1999. 242!/57.

Galligan, Brian, and Winsome Roberts. *Australian Citizenship*. Carlton, Vic.: Melbourne UP, 2004.

"Globalization and Liberalization" Prospects of New World Order – Dr. A.K. Ojha, *Third Concept – An International Journal of Ideas*, Aug, 2002.

Goldberg, David H. 'Multicultural Conditions.' *Multiculturalism: A Critical Reader*. Ed. David H. Goldberg. Boston: Blackwell, 1994.

Gutmann, Amy. 'Introduction.' *Multiculturalism: Examining the Politics of Recognition*. Ed. Amy Gutmann. Princeton, NJ: Princeton UP, 1994. 3-23.

Gutmann, Amy, and Dennis Thompson. *Democracy and Disagreement*, Cambridge, MA: Harvard UP, 1996.

Habermas, Jurgen. *Moral Consciousness and Communicative Action* . Trans. Christian Lenhardt and Shierry W. Nicholsen. Cambridge, MA: MIT P, 1990.

——, 'Struggles for Recognition in the Democratic Constitutional State.' Multiculturalism: Examining the Politics of Recognition. Ed. Amy Gutmann. Princeton, NJ: Princeton UP, 1994. 107!/48.

——. *Between Facts and Norms: Contributions to a Discourse Theory of Law and Democracy*. Trans. William Rehg. Cambridge, MA: MITP, 1996.

Hacker, A. (1965) 'Power to do What'? In I.L. Horowitz (ed.) *The New Sociology*, New York, Oxford University Press.

Hage, Ghassan. *Against Paranoid Nationalism: Searching for Hope in a Shrinking Society*. Annandale: Pluto, 2003.

Hirst, John. 'More or Less Diverse.' *Unity and Diversity: A National Conversation (The Barton Lectures)*. Ed. Helen Irving. Sydney: ABC, 2001, 110-29.

Horne, Donald. *Public Culture: An Argument with the Future*. London: Pluto, 1994.

—— 'Something Fishy in the Mainstream?' *Unity and Diversity: A National Conversation (The Barton Lectures)*. Ed. Helen Irving. Sydney: ABC, 2001. 1-19.

Hudson, Wayne. 'Differential Citizenship.' *Rethinking Australian Citizenship*. Eds. Wayne Hudson and John Kane. New York: Cambridge UP, 2000. 15-25.

Jayasuriya, Laksiri. *Immigration and Multiculturalism in Australia* . Nedlands, WA: School of Social Work and Social Administration, U of Western Australia, 1997.

Joppke, Christian. 'Immigration Challenges the Nation-State.' *Challenge to the Nation-State: Immigration in Western Europe and the United States*. Ed. Christian Joppke. Oxford: Oxford UP, 1998. 5-48.

——, 'Multicultural Citizenship: A Critique.' *European Journal of Sociology* 42.2 (2001): 431-47.

Joppke, Christian, and Steven Lukes. 'Introduction: Multicultural Questions.' *Multicultural Questions* . Eds. Christian Joppke and Steven Lukes. Oxford: Oxford UP, 1999. 1-26.

Jupp, James. 'Does Australia Need a National Identity?' *Australian Identities*. Ed. David Day. Melbourne: Australian Scholarly Publishing, 1998. 223-36.

Kalantzis, Mary. 'Civic Pluralism and Total Globalisation.' Republics of Ideas: Republicanism, Culture, Visual Arts. Eds. Brad Bucklet and John Conomos. Annandale: Pluto and Artspace Visual Arts Centre, 2001a. 110-23.

——. 'Recognising Diversity.' *Reconciliation, Multiculturalism, Identities: Difficult Dialogues, Sensible Solutions*. Eds. Mary Kalantzis and Bill Cope. Altona, Vic.: Common Ground Publishing, 2001b. 11-25.

Kane, John. 'Communitarianism and Citizenship.' *Rethinking Australian Citizenship*. Eds. Wayne Hudson and John Kane. New York: Cambridge UP, 2000. 215!/ 30.

Kelly, Duncan. 'Multicultural Citizenship: The Limitations of Liberal Democracy.' *Political Quarterly* 71.1 (2000): 31-41.

Kelly, Paul J. '"Dangerous Liaisons": Parekh and "Oakeshottian" Multiculturalism.' *Political Quarterly* 72.4 (2001): 428-36.

Koopmans, Ruud, and Paul Statham. 'Challenging the Liberal Nation-State? Postnationalism, Multiculturalism, and the Collective Claims Making of Migrants and Ethnic Minorities in Britain and Germany.' *American Journal of Sociology* 105.3 (1999): 652-96.

Kukathas, Chandran. 'Liberalism and Multiculturalism: The Politics of Indifference.' *Political Theory* 26.5 (1998): 686-99.

Kymlicka, Will. *Multicultural Citizenship: A Liberal Theory of Minority Rights*. Oxford: Oxford UP, 1995.

——, 'A North American View.' (Review symposium: report of the Commission on the Future of Multi-Ethnic Britain: UK, North American and Continental European perspectives). *Journal of Ethnic and Migration Studies* 26.4 (2000): 723-33.

Laborde, Cecile. 'From Constitutional to Civic Patriotism.' *British Journal of Political Science* 32 (2002): 591-612.

Love, Peter. 'National Identity and Citizenship.' *Australian Identities*. Ed. David Day. Melbourne: Australian Scholarly Publishing, 1998, 212-21.

Marshall, T.H. (1934) "Social Class – A Preliminary Analysis.

Marshall, Thomas H. Class, *Citizenship and Social Development: Essays by T. H. Marshall*. New York: Anchor Books, 1964.

Marshal, T.H. (1950) *Citizenship and Social Class*.

Mascovici, Claudia, *Gender and Citizenship: Two Dialectics of Subject*, Rowman and Littlefield, 2000.

McRoberts, Kenneth. *Misconceiving Canada: The Struggle for National Unity*. Toronto: Oxford UP, 1997.

Miller, David. *On Nationality*. Oxford: Clarendon P, 1995.

National Multicultural Advisory Council (NMAC). *Multicultural Australia: The Next Steps, Towards and Beyond 2000*. Canberra: AGPS, 1995.

——, *Multiculturalism for a New Century: Towards Inclusiveness*. Canberra: AGPS, 1999.

Office of Multicultural Affairs (OMA). *National Agenda for a Multicultural Australia*. Canberra: AGPS, 1989.

Parekh, Bhikhu. 'Dilemmas of a Multicultural Theory of Citizenship.' *Constellations* 4.1 (1997): 54-62.

——. *Rethinking Multiculturalism*. Basingstoke: Macmillan, 2000.

Parkin, F. (1971): *Class Inequality and Political Order*, London, Paladin.

Rawls, John. *The Idea of Public Reason Revisited (with The Law of Peoples)* . Cambridge, MA: Harvard UP, 1999.

Ray, B.N., *Citizenship in a Globalised World*, New Delhi, Kaveri Books, 2007.

Rockefeller, Steven C. 'Comment.' *Multiculturalism: Examining the Politics of Recognition*. Ed. Amy Gutmann. Princeton, NJ: Princeton UP, 1994. 87-101.

Shabani, Omid A. P. 'Who's Afraid of Constitutional Patriotism? The Binding Source of Citizenship in Constitutional States.' *Social Theory and Practice* 28.3 (2002): 419-44.

Shachar, Ayelet. 'The Paradox of Multicultural

Vulnerability: Individual Rights, Identity Groups, and the State.' *Multicultural Questions*. Eds. Christian Joppke and Steven Lukes. Oxford: Oxford UP, 1999. 87-111.

Slim, Brite, *Gender and Citizenship*, ed, Illustrated, Cambridge University Press, 2000.

Smith, Rodney. *Australian Political Culture*. Frenchs Forest: Pearson Education, 2001.

Smolicz, Jerzy J. 'Australia: From Migrant Country to Multicultural Nation.' *International Migration Review* 31.1 (1997): 171-86.

Spinner-Halev, Jeff. 'Cultural Pluralism and Partial Citizenship.' *Multicultural Questions* . Eds. Christian Joppke and Steven Lukes. Oxford: Oxford UP, 1999. 65-86.

Stratton, Hugh. *Race Daze: Australia in Identity Crisis*. Sydney: Pluto, 1998.

Tamir, Yael. *Liberal Nationalism*. Princeton, NJ: Princeton UP, 1993.

Taylor, Charles. 'The Politics of Recognition.' *Multiculturalism: Examining the Politics of Recognition*. Ed. Amy Gutmann. Princeton, NJ: Princeton UP, 1994. 25-74.

Tully, James. Strange Multiplicity: Constitutionalism in *an Age of Diversity*. Cambridge: Cambridge UP, 1995.

Turner, B.S. (1986) *Citizenship and Capitalism*, London, Allen and Unwin.

Turner, B.S. (1994) *Citizenship and Social Theory*.

Uhr, John. *Deliberative Democracy: The Changing Place of Parliament*. Cambridge and Melbourne: Cambridge UP, 1998.

Webber, Jeremy. *Re-imagining Canada: Culture, Community and the Canadian Constitution*. Kingston and Montreal: MacGill-Queen's UP, 1994.

Weber, M. (1925) (1971) *General Economic History*, New Brunswick, Transaction Books.

Young, Iris M. 'Polity and Group Difference: A Critique of the Ideal of Universal Citizenship.' *Ethics* 99 (1989): 250-74.

Index